GRIEF TALKS

Thoughts on Life, Death, and Positive Healing

Jenny Filush-Glaze, M.Ed., LPC

Woodson Knowles Publishing Group
301 Lee Road 15
Auburn, AL 36830

https://www.wkpublishing.org

1. Grief Support 2. Inspiration

ISBN: 978-0-99806032-3

First Edition

Cover photographs by Jenny Filush-Glaze
Cover Design by Iris Saya Miller

Contents

Remember the Children

Living and Grieving

A Way Forward

Foreword

The pain of losing someone is a feeling that we will all face. Grief is typically thought of as an emotional response to a loss, however, it often has physical, cognitive, and social consequences. In *Grief Talks: Thoughts on Life, Death, and Positive Healing*, Jenny Filush-Glaze uses her vast background in clinical counseling, crisis management, and education to tackle the subject and provide the reader with different perspectives on how to deal with grief through awareness and support.

This topic has been a passion for Jenny and she has dedicated her professional career to educating patients, families, colleagues, and the community to help them better understand and cope with grief. Jenny is often a guest speaker on hospice, death and dying, and child and adult grief for classes at Auburn University. Her educational efforts extend to training school teachers and hospice staff in identifying children who are grieving and how to support them, and she works in crisis intervention in school and community settings during times of sudden and violent deaths.

Jenny provides support through weekly newspaper columns, internet blogs, and magazine articles in an effort to reach people who are unable to find support or who are unwilling to attend support groups after their loss. She also reaches out to children whom she considers to be the "forgotten mourners." In 2005, she founded Camp Good Grief, a day camp for kids who have lost loved ones, which provides children an opportunity to be with other children while assisting them in expressing their feelings and learning coping mechanisms that will help with their healing.

I have known and worked with Jenny for eleven years in my role as hospice medical director where she serves as a Grief and Bereavement Coordinator. I have seen firsthand her compassion, empathy, and love for the grieving patients and their families. She is gifted at moderating open support groups and meeting within the homes of families who have lost loved ones. Through her writings

i

and face-to-face interactions, she reminds us that everyone is a person with hopes and dreams, wishes, feelings and fears.

Enjoy *Grief Talks* as Jenny provides insight on a sometimes painful topic in a way that will allow you to reflect, give you tools to assist in dealing with losses, and to smile at times along the way.

John A. Abrams, MD
Hospice Medical Director, Hospice Compassus
Auburn, AL

Preface

Many years ago, I felt called to reach out to those who had suffered the death of a loved one and offer them the support that I felt had been severely lacking within our community. At the time, I was repeatedly told that, "no one wants to talk about that kind of stuff, it's too sad," and I was quickly shuffled out the door and sent on my way. When this occurred, I would become extremely frustrated and wonder aloud why people couldn't see the need for ongoing grief support, and then I would stand taller, strengthen my resolve and try harder to find a solution. When I say that grief is a "passion" of mine, I do not say it lightly. I feel strongly that grief awareness is an issue that needs more focus within our communities in order to assist those who walk along a path filled with a myriad of emotions, while feeling as if they are all alone or that something is wrong with them because of how they are experiencing grief.

When the opportunity to start writing a grief column for the local newspaper fell into my lap, I jumped at the chance to further my mission of bringing grief awareness and support to those who were hurting and to the family and friends who support them. Agreement was reached to start a biweekly column in order to "test the waters" and see if the community would be receptive to the subject matter, and then a decision would be made after a few months to determine if the column would continue. For a year and a half, the column flourished and as positive feedback soared and interest became evident, the decision was made to run the column weekly. Imagine my joy! Every week I would now have the opportunity to reach others and offer support for the grieving without them having to be physically present in order to receive the support. Currently, the column is running weekly in two different newspapers. Because of my daily work amongst those who are either anticipating loss or who are currently on their grief journey, and the inspiration I receive from them, I have been encouraged to gather these columns in book form.

I do not expect that every column will speak to you or inspire you in some way. But, I do hope that you will find comfort, solace or even inspiration of your own from something that you read, and that you will then be able to take it to heart and perhaps assist someone else who may be just starting along their grief journey. I always invite people to share their stories, to express their feelings, and to recognize that grief is a normal part of life. The feelings are real and deserve to be validated. Often that is all someone needs—just one time someone telling them that they will be okay and that they will make it beyond the initial stages of devastation.

My goal is to open up these lines of communication and keep them going, to offer support to anyone who is open to talking about their loss, and to welcome them into the arms of healing and encourage them along the way. This book is dedicated to all of those who said that grief was "not something that needed to be talked about" and to all of those who appreciate and support grief awareness and the need for supporting the bereaved.

Lastly, to my parents, my extended family, and to my "Happy Family" for always encouraging me to put my passion on paper. May this be just the beginning of the journey.

Jenny Filush-Glaze

Sorrow and Joy

"When you are sorrowful look again in your heart,
and you shall see that in truth you are weeping
for that which has been your delight."

—Kahlil Gibran

Grief Relief

As I was setting out to write the first column on grief and the difficult journey it often takes us on, I was focused on a word that would instantly bring us together. I chose the word "WELCOME" because many people on a grief journey no longer feel "WELCOME" to share their emotions, express what they need from their friends and family members, or even attend a local support group. Grief changes us. It can take hold and render us useless for days, months, and even years at a time, and when this occurs, we struggle to find our way. My goal for this column is to share real issues and real stories from our community about the way we grieve. In my role as a bereavement counselor, I have found that the best support I can give to those who have experienced loss is to validate their feelings and let them know that not only are their feelings real, but that they are often shared by others. With this said, I would like to formally invite you to be a part of this journey—TOGETHER. Please come inside and know that you are safe here, that you are "WELCOME."

For those who are grieving or who have experienced a traumatic loss, either anticipated or unexpected, this is your chance to be a part of an open support group without having to be physically present. It has become readily apparent in our society that those seeking support are often looked upon as being weak or lacking in the ability to handle adversity. People voice that they are hesitant to ask for help because they are afraid of being judged or of being told that they are not handling things the right way. In all honesty, what *is* the right way?

Does someone who is grieving really have all the answers, and do people who have never experienced a loss have the right to tell us how we should be grieving? The truth is simple in that grief is as individualized as a human thumbprint. We may have some similarities and some overlap, however, our relationship with the person who has died is ours and ours alone. Asking for support is actually a sign of strength that not many of us have taken advantage of in today's world.

As a society, it is important that we focus more on being PRESENT for others and actually listening to them—not be so quick to offer advice or pass judgment. In our haste to provide comfort, to ease the pain or to "fix things," we sometimes forget to listen. Listening is hard and can be painful.

A casual statement made may cause someone to feel lost or confused, and an absent action may elicit feelings of abandonment. Grief is a tricky obstacle that all of us will face at some point in our lives—some much sooner than others. How we face that grief within ourselves and how we pay it forward to others goes a long way in helping people progress along their grief journey. Consider exploring more about how loss makes us feel and how we can be supportive of others in our community. Unfortunately, loss is a part of life, and instead of feeling LOST amongst our peers during this most difficult time, let us FIND and support one another—let us make the effort to reach out and say, "WELCOME."

Stumbling Delicately Through Life

As the world moves swiftly around us, we rarely take the time to stop and think about how our actions may influence others. We bounce from project to project, rush from one red light to the next, never once glancing behind at all that we have passed or even left behind. When did life become so hurried? When did we become so focused on achieving greatness that we lost sight of all the real things that matter?

Some of the most inspiring quotes I have come across lately are the ones that talk about not focusing on making mistakes. Mistakes are part of human nature and I am of the opinion that these missteps, these "take backs" or "do-overs," simply mold and fashion us into the shape we were meant to become. Stumbling through life with our eyes wide open—taking a long, hard glance at where we have been and where we want to be, is part of the forward movement. If we are fearful of losing, of not being perfect, of falling apart in the face of adversity, well, then we are probably meant to maintain some level of mediocrity. Life becomes stagnant when we stay still and never make the effort to improve ourselves by venturing into the scariness of the unknown. However, it should be noted that once we stumble and fall, whether it is a minor scrape or a flat-on-your-face catastrophe, if we would but sit quietly and listen, we might notice that life is still going on around us.

Life simply is and always will be a force of nature that can create chaos or can help us to see that we took part in creating that chaos. Sometimes, stumbling and falling is part of the healing process. When we take time to reflect on our actions and what caused the effect, we can hear the words of wisdom we may have previously ignored, and the voice of wisdom can wrap gently around us and pull us tightly to its bosom. Only then can we evidence change and create a new path of decision making, a new idea of learning.

So why stumble delicately? Why not bull rush head first into every decision, knocking over any and everything in your path? Because by stumbling delicately, you are allowing yourself time to slow down and appreciate life. The frenetic pace of choice and actions once again becomes manageable as everything eases and now trots along beside you at the momentum you have established. Time slows and becomes an ally instead of an adversary.

Now, when you place one foot in front of the other, making a cognizant choice to examine the living and breathing animal that is your being, you are in control of the outcome. Remember, mistakes help to shape us but only if we are open to accepting that these mistakes were made in order to teach us life's lessons. If we are closed to this knowledge, if we continue to stumble blindly and maddeningly without care or concern, then we are risking the loss of all that we could have hoped to gain.

From early childhood we are taught to clean up spills, erase mistakes and start over. We grow up with the expectation that we have to be the best in order to achieve the highest honors. Blessed are we that had the teachers who praised not only our accomplishments and our achievements, but also gently pointed out our mistakes and helped us learn from them. They taught us that failure was a part of life and that pushing through that failure really was a better measure of how we could secure our future.

This strength, this fortitude changed perceptions and established a new way of thinking; one of conquering adversity in spite of others trying to keep us down. By stumbling through life delicately, we can finally take the time to notice that we are strong, that we do have presence and that we do matter. With life awareness, we can now take notice of the old man in the wheelchair stuck on the side of the road, or the dog who is wandering lost along the highway. With this new awareness, we are more likely to stop and offer assistance because we are now looking both forward and backward, taking the time to be present for others.

We have chosen to become a part of life, even if we don't always have all the answers, and this is a positive thing. For when we take time for others, and stumble delicately, we can now look at the bruising from our many falls and watch as it changes colors and fades into the beginning of a new healing, a new life that is no longer delicate. It is through this process that we become strong; accepting that faults are a reality in this life and if we are open to learning from them instead of avoiding them by stumbling quickly and without abandon, that is when we realize that we have truly lived.

Finding Your Peace Place

Peace. It is a simple word and yet, after a death occurs, it is a word that seems to be elusive in our minds. We long for a time to sit still and reflect on the loss of our loved one and look back over the years and memories we have shared with them. However, more often than not, what happens instead, is that we are inundated with trials and tribulations, phone calls and tracking down of documents, or long wait times on the phone with customer service representatives. All of this contributes to the chaos and frustration we feel when we are simply trying to grieve and are many times delayed due to the inability to create a space for our mourning.

One of the most important and essential things we can do for ourselves when grieving is to identify time that can be spent on reflection. We need to be able to monitor our inner world and recalibrate our thoughts and emotions into some semblance of order that makes sense to us. Grief can cause disorganization and loss of focus, which is normal. Many times, people will say that they "cannot think straight" let alone grieve because of all that is going on around them, not to mention all the expectations that people have for them as well. When this occurs, it is recommended that you allow time for yourself for healing. What can be healing and how do we go about finding peace?

Last week, while standing against the powerful waves of the Atlantic Ocean, my seven-year-old niece asked me, "Why do people go to the ocean when they are sad?" I had just a moment to think about this before the next wave came crashing in and took us both under the water, depositing us a few feet further down the shoreline. I realized that grief is oftentimes just like that wave—powerful and towering, too big to stay standing on our feet, even if we had all the strength in the world. Like grief, that wave topples us and spins us underwater, leaving us feeling disoriented and lost when we resurface. After a moment, we are able to glimpse the shore and reorient ourselves to place and time. How many of us have felt this way after the death of our loved one?

Peace can be found at the ocean, in the mountains, in our faith and in ourselves if we allow it to make its way. It is not easy to give ourselves permission to grieve, and not all of us are able to travel to find the gift that peace can bring to our hearts. However, I do know that the ocean is a very healing and centering place to be—whether we are sad, happy, or just in need of some personal time. People do, in fact, go to the ocean when they are sad. Something about the sound of the waves, the screech of the gulls, the taste and feel of the salt water on your skin soothes the pain that rides within us. If only our hurt and pain could hitchhike on that wave and ride out into the depths of the ocean never to be seen again, or our tears could be washed away forever. Instead, I see our grief floating alongside us, caressing our anguish in its healing waters.

As I stood with my niece, her sweet little hand held tightly in mine, she looked up at me and said, "Please don't let me go ... that wave was big and scary." I squeezed her hand reassuringly and told her I would never let her go, that she could trust me to keep her safe." I knew in that moment that I was releasing some unresolved grief of my own, not letting it go, but finding some much needed healing and inner peace. Staring down the next wave, I realized that you never really know how strong you are until being strong is the only choice. I choose to ride the wave where grief takes me.

The Search for Balance

As we look ahead to a new year, I find it most important to take some time to reflect upon ourselves; to turn inward and find the balance that we need in our lives. All too often, we discover that we are run down or exhausted from all the tasks and daily requirements we face. Maybe we have been involved in some long-term care giving or maybe we have been walking the long and difficult path of grieving. Too many times, people look at the month of January as the month of "new beginnings" and "do overs." However, just as many people look at it as a quiet and treacherous month—one that is dark and lonely, cold and rainy, leaving us feeling melancholic or lugubrious.

As a grief counselor, it is necessary for me to find balance. Don't get me wrong, it is not the easiest thing in the world to do, but it is of utmost importance. In fact, I often discover that I am overwhelmed, stressed, exhausted or irritable. People ask me all the time how I am able to do the work that I do, and all I can tell them is that: (1) It is a calling, and (2) I have to work hard at taking care of myself so that I can have the daily strength to be there for others when they need me. Living life every day is taxing and can wear our defenses down. Facing death and experiencing the pain of loss is devastating and it can create a storm that is so forceful that it can knock the wind out of our sails and throw us off balance for long periods of time.

Recently, I read an article about the importance of recognizing that we need both light and dark in our lives. There may be times when life feels full of promise and light, where we are hopeful and we maintain that "anything is possible" attitude. But, then there are those times when it appears that darkness has descended, and light seems elusive and unattainable. Many people, while talking about their grief journey, have shared that they know there will be "light at the end of the tunnel"—they are just waiting to get there. Sometimes it really does take time to adjust and refocus to our new lives, to balance the light and the dark. Having people surround us, that love and nurture us, can go a long way in helping us see that sometimes we need the darkness just as much as we need the light.

After the holidays are over, the anxiety of spending holidays without our loved ones, and the clamor and tension of having "made it through" this most difficult time, we should be prepared for yet another hurdle. Many know it as "The Winter Blues," and I can adamantly state that I have honestly always dreaded the month of January. My approach to this month has always been filled with reproach and disdain, counting down the days until that horrid month is behind me. However, this year, I plan to approach the New Year with a heightened sense of balance, knowing that this month could offer me the opportunity to do some personal reflection and self-discovery. Instead of hibernating and avoiding, I am going to focus on the fact that we are not promised each day and therefore I plan to approach each day as the gift it was meant to be—to learn more about myself and how I can be more available to those who may require my assistance. For me, every single day I am faced with life and death, a new beginning and a new ending. I am grateful for the light and the darkness that resides within my soul. By embracing both, I believe it is possible to create a healthy balance, one that can replace the darkest shadows with the brilliant radiance that lives within us all.

Be Your Own Pilot

I remember as a child, that if I ever had a question that I needed an answer to, and my parents didn't have the information, I would pour through encyclopedias or make a trip to the library to find what I needed. Today, with all the technology in place, we can simply pull out our handheld devices and "Google" it. Information from all over the world shows up in a matter of seconds and gives us instantaneous knowledge to satisfy our curiosity and need for enlightenment. However, when we are grieving, there really isn't a "How To" manual to flip through and learn all the particulars—the "ins and outs." Sure, you can find all kinds of information on grieving and some of it is extremely helpful, but when it comes right down to it, grieving isn't really something you learn about in a book or on the internet, it is something you live. And, by living it, that is when you learn something useful.

Too many times I have heard people say that they feel "stuck" in their grief. I know I have written about that before, but I think the point I would like to make here is different entirely. Sometimes we are stuck because the grief is simply disabling, leaving us feeling numb or immobilized. But, other times, we stay "stuck" in our grief because it has become easier to do this than it would be to venture forward. Don't get me wrong—I don't necessarily think this is a conscious choice, that we are willing to stay in the "pit of despair"; instead it is more that staying in that dormant space has become comfortable. When we are in that space, we can connect to our grief, we can feel closer to our loved ones who have left us behind, and we can truly mourn. Stepping outside of that space is very difficult; it begins to signal to others that we are healing and moving forward in our grief journey. For some, this step forward is very frightening and uncomfortable, often forcing a quick retreat—back to the "pit of despair."

Other people talk about how they move forward each day just going through the motions, never taking the time to think about their actions or their intentions. They describe a "grief haze" of lost time, forgotten memories and an inability to focus. Today I would like for you to think about the importance of taking control of your own grief—to be your own pilot if you will. Grief is uncomfortable, it always has been and always will be. Try to embrace your grief as an experience that you will undoubtedly learn from, even though it is a life lesson that we would rather not have to face. Instead of spending so much time in our "pit of despair," let us strive to step outside of that space and gain some control back of our life. When death occurs, life spirals out of control in so many different ways and directions. However, once some time passes, those spirals and out-of-control things should settle down and become more manageable. How do we manage our grief?

Again, it is about becoming our own pilot. Some of us visualize joining our loved ones and choose to live each day more focused on the day that we will see them again instead of looking at each day as a gift, a gift that is never promised. Time is lost and it is time that is needed to heal, but there does come a point when we simply need to grab the wheel and choose to fly instead of careen off course. Let us focus on mindfulness and our ability to influence our own grief journey. As we continue on each day, think about how you would like to fly alongside others instead of flying solo, and maybe then, we can truly journey together.

Rediscovering Joy

Everywhere we look, there are people laughing and sharing in the delights of life and in each other. Couples are holding hands, children are smiling and playing, and pets are dancing to the tune of dreams only they can envision. What happens when life comes to a screeching halt and all that joy is suddenly taken from us? Where does it go and how do we find it again?

Many people often share that their biggest fear after the death of a loved one is that they will "never be happy again" that their "life is over." What I gently tell them, is that "Yes, your life will never be the same again—it won't, but that doesn't mean that happiness is unattainable." Sometimes I happen to catch a quick glimpse of hope in their eyes, a flash of genuine need to rediscover the joy that once lived in their hearts. But, more often than not, I see eyes full of disbelief and confusion, and even more heartbreaking, the pinpoint stare of fear that there is nothing left in this world worth living for.

As a grief counselor, it is an everyday challenge to listen to the weight of others' hurt and pain; lifting them up and helping them see that hope is there, just lying dormant for the time when we are ready to once again listen to the birds singing. The biggest obstacle at times is the inability to see that we are in fact entitled to finding happiness in our lives—because it is human nature to respond as if we no longer deserve it; that we are "supposed to be sad and alone." To a fault, society places expectations upon us, dictating how we are supposed to grieve and for how long. If others' thoughts and behaviors influence how we feel, how can we expect to rediscover joy and move forward in *our* grief journey?

To begin, it is essential that we realize that we can never take away how others feel—those are their feelings and they are genuine and real. What we need to do is help them process through those feelings and gently guide them forward in their way of thinking. Being positive and supportive of our friends and family members who are grieving is a sure-fire way to assure them that you are trustworthy of hearing what they have to say. Processing feelings, peeling back the layers of that onion and gaining speed toward the delicate center, is painful. However, the work is necessary and the end results are often rewarding. To witness the rediscovery of joy in someone's life, when they realize that they have finally emerged on the other side of a very painful journey, is one of the greatest and most amazing gifts. It is an honor and a privilege to be a part of one's journey; to hold their hand as they walk across the pitfalls of life and watch the dissipation of that terrible darkness. Joy is part of life, it truly is, even after death.

Finding Strength

"We acquire the strength we have overcome."

—Ralph Waldo Emerson

A Definition of Strength

"I've always thought I was a strong person. What is wrong with me?" Time after time, I am faced with this desperate plea from those who have experienced the death of a loved one. Their eyes are full of tears; their faces are struggling to maintain composure, only to crumple beneath the weight of a grief that is more than they can bear. Too many times, people confuse the word "strength" with "being strong." When anticipating the death, or shortly after the death occurs, friends and family will approach us with the dreaded words, "Stay strong." The words themselves are meant to be encouraging or uplifting, however, the horrible truth is that they can sometimes be limiting and oppressive. How so?

Think about this. If I am told repeatedly by people who love and care about me that I need to "stay strong," it sends me a message that I cannot share my grief with others. It tells me that I must hide my grief away, closed behind a door, lying dormant just beneath the surface of a false smile. My ready response becomes one of "I'm fine," so as to avoid letting others down. This is an injustice to those who grieve and mourn. If we are taught to repress our feelings, to hold them in and "be strong," then it is a no-brainer that we will feel like we have failed in our individual grief journey if we break down and cry in front of others. When did our grief, our loss, our pain become all about living for other people? Shouldn't we be able to have moments of sadness, to cry when a wave of despair hits us unexpectedly? In short, the answer is an overwhelming yes.

Truthfully, it takes "strength" to be able to express how we are feeling to others. Strength is something that resides within us, that we draw from when it seems like we cannot possibly drag another foot forward in our grief journey. Strength helps us to process our loss; it guides us in decision making and gives us the courage to face each day, even when we don't think that we can. Giving verbal cues to our friends and family, letting them know what we need or don't need from them, requires strength. Strength is about our inner ability to live; it is a "want to." Having to be "strong," so that others will feel better about how we are grieving, or so they will not worry about us, is simply a defense mechanism, and one that we use often. It is human nature to say, "I'm fine," even when the inside of us is screaming with hurt and pain. Why is it that the mentality of "take care of others first," continues even after the death occurs thus placing our needs on the backburner? Why do we feel the need to make sure everyone else is okay and outwardly ignore the desire to share our grief with others?

In short, I think that we can both "be strong" and show "strength" in our grief journey. The key is being able to recognize that you are strong by simply living; that strength is part of what brings you to live another day. Don't misunderstand, outwardly showing a strong sense of character can be very important and is a very acceptable coping mechanism that can guide us through grief. My point is, if we choose to present to others that we are strong because it helps us to survive—fine. However, if we are encouraged to wear the mask of "I'm fine," in order to help others cope with our sadness, this becomes the travesty, and true strength is lost.

Facing Our Fears

The words death and dying often bring about some of our deepest and darkest fears. They symbolize an ending of life and many times an end to our hopes and dreams as well. It is no wonder that death is seen as a "taboo" subject; one that is often avoided and only confronted when it is absolutely necessary. Even doctors and trained physicians or specialists tend to avoid this topic at times because they know what the end result brings— loss and heartache, grief and pain.

As a bereavement counselor, I have the privilege to be a part of death in every way, form and fashion. I am able to sit bedside and hold someone's hand, waiting for the last breath. I am called in for emergencies, when a death is sudden or violent to help those who are left behind. At other times, I come in after a death to help validate feelings and encourage hope. To me, death is not scary or something that I fear because I face it on an every day basis. My family often tires of the way that I view death and how I am constantly talking about the way death can either draw a family closer together or tear them apart. Because it seems so familiar to me, I speak about death as if it was an actual being, hoping that others will become more aware of all the issues that death and dying brings within our family systems and community.

It is okay to fear death, as that is human nature. From the moment we are born, our lives are focused on the living and the breathing, the exploring and the creating of life. We don't take the time to stop and think about how each day is never promised or that tragedy could be waiting right around the corner. Why would we? It doesn't make any sense to worry about something that might not happen until we are well into our senior years, however, when the opportunity does come to address it and discuss it, it is my hope that we would all face our fears about death and have an open and honest conversation.

I am terrified of heights and there is no classical conditioning that could be done to alleviate this fear. Recently I was in the mountains, scaling rocks and treacherous pathways, rejuvenated by the crisp, cool air. I climbed platforms and traversed to hidden waterfalls, but all the while, there were times when I simply could go no further due to my debilitating fear. With grief, I often think about how those newly bereaved feel—the fear of being alone; the fear of losing one's identity; the fear of financial concerns or changed relationships. Those fears are valid and very real. They sometimes grip our hearts and minds and refuse to let us move forward until we are able to work through some of our journey and face those fears head on. Grief is scary. At times, it can cause heart palpitations and chest pain (often mimicking a heart attack); at other times it can cause memory loss and confusion. We feel afraid, unable to put our next foot forward because we are uncertain of what the next step may bring. But then, something miraculous happens; we wake up one morning and realize that we have moved down the road and didn't even realize it; that we have taken steps forward and faced some of our deepest fears and conquered them.

It is important to remember that facing our fears is difficult. For me, there were times when I was able to reach the pinnacle of a mountain and view the absolutely stunning display of beauty and nature around me. However, there were times when I also knew I had gone as far as I could that day; that some areas were just off limits to me. As with a grief journey, I had wonderful family support encouraging me along the way that helped me reach heights I thought I would never achieve. At times, they were disappointed when I wasn't able to reach the top. But, I know they were there for me and were proud of all that I had accomplished. Death is a mountain that we will all have to face and even climb some day. When it is our turn, it is my hope that we will be able to reach the tallest peak, take a deep breath, look at our surroundings and know that we had the strength to embrace our deepest fears.

Honoring Life After Death—Your Own

Despair. In the opinion of many, no word can better describe the absolute agony that the death of a loved one brings. When grieving and contemplating our loss, we often feel overwhelmed by the hopelessness we feel for a life that is forever changed. We lose sight of our purpose, our strength, and sometimes even our will to live. It is not uncommon for those who are in the beginning stages of their grief journey to express the desire "to die." The anguish they are facing, living in a world that now seems empty without their loved one, is too much to bear. All around them, life goes on, and the burden of living becomes greater. Feelings of despair now turn to hopelessness and thoughts of suicide become rampant. Is this normal?

One of the things, of which I would like to assure you, is that thoughts of suicide while we are grieving, are not at all unusual. Keep in mind that it is during this time that our thoughts and emotions are raw. We are often focused on the belief that things will never get better and that to go on living would be pointless. Sometimes, we might be afraid to voice these feelings to others because we don't want to be judged. However, it should be pointed out again that many people experience these same exact thoughts with the same level of despair. Sometimes, sharing these thoughts with others who are also grieving, helps to validate for us that our feelings are real and normal. To hear others tell us that they experienced some of the same thoughts lets us know that we are not alone and that there is hope to make it beyond this most difficult part of our journey.

Remember this one important fact: There is a vast difference between thinking about suicide and actually acting upon those thoughts. Most of us "feel" like we want to die, however we never intend to act upon it. It's just that it is so difficult to contemplate life moving forward when we feel so empty inside. Truthfully, those thoughts and feelings will eventually subside and we will move beyond feeling suicidal into a different stage of mourning. Nothing is more validating than being able to look back at this stage in your life and know that you were at "rock bottom" and didn't wish to live; but then seeing that you made it through and that hope once again entered your life. It is true that time heals. It is also true that grief means you will go from feeling like you want to die to recognizing the fact that you are indeed still living.

In closing, when the darkness starts to dissipate, the clouds begin to lift, and you are able to "breathe again," life becomes a new journey. The death of our loved one actually winds up giving us the strength to recognize that our lives are important, and through the despair, we are given the strength to pull ourselves out of its grip. In the beginning, it doesn't seem possible; however, as we continue on our path, we realize that we *are* able to once again live. Even though our loved ones are no longer physically present, we owe it to them and to ourselves to travel a new path, to take hold of the reins of our life and begin a new chapter. Making new memories while cherishing the old ones is a bold statement to others; it shouts that we are alive and that we are well worth the wait that it has taken for us to get there.

Live Like You Are Dying

After reading the last page, I sat back and closed my eyes and said good-bye to the characters I had grown to love in the telling of a wonderful story. It was a book about life, and it was a book about death. But, most importantly, it was about learning how to live your life even when you don't feel worthy of living. Many times throughout the reading of this novel, I found myself stopping and thinking about the characters' dialogue. And, just as often, I could hear and feel the pain through all of the words left unspoken.

To me, this experience sums up what so often happens during the grieving process. At times, we are quick to address issues at hand and are eager to spend as much time with our loved ones as possible. But, at other times, we find ourselves stuck in the avoidant mode of "if I don't talk about it, it doesn't exist." In the novel that I read, a seventy-year-old woman was diagnosed with pancreatic cancer and was determined to accomplish many of her life goals before the cancer "took her out." She was active, spunky, and fiercely set in her ways, making sure that others respected her wishes and allowed her to devote her time and energies to making a difference for others. By doing this, she set an example that inspired many to later pick up where she left off. But for the time being, her days were to be spent within the borders of healing energies that consumed her every action.

More times than I can count, I was moved by the adult son who found himself conflicted and angry about his mother's diagnosis. He chided himself for thinking about how much his life was going to be affected when she was gone and felt guilty about avoiding conversations about her impending death. Like the elephant in the room that everyone tiptoes around, he struggled with people dancing around the difficult topics and wanted to scream at the top of his lungs that his mother was dying. And yet, he sensed that this would not be helpful to his mother and he wanted to make sure she was comfortable and that her dignity was treasured and preserved. His constant battle reminded me of so many families who have the same thoughts and feelings about preparing for death. We all tend to think and say the same things and yet having those discussions seems hurtful, like in preparing for their death, we are saying that we don't care.

And, even though we may feel this way, it is evident that many who are dying choose to initiate those conversations, even if we are not ready. This is often painful to watch because in our frantic unpreparedness, we have only to simply acknowledge that at this point, it is not about us—it is about them. In choosing to live their lives and make the most out of each day, they want to share with us that they are accepting of their fate (no doubt having already gone through the "it's not fair" and "why me" scenarios) and are not only preparing themselves, but are also preparing us for our future life without them. At the time, we may want to run away and avoid every single bit of this, but later, after the death occurs, we are able to see these conversations as the gifts they truly are and feel the gratefulness as it explodes within our minds and bodies for having a loved one so precious.

In living like we are dying, we are choosing to embrace the world and all it has to offer. We stare death in the face and tell it "not today" and then quietly but effectively continue about our business. Not all of us have the luxury of anticipating that death is coming, but if we do, it is important to be respectful of each moment and to be willing to dance around the edges of our comfort zone. Death is not comfortable and it is often filled with all kinds of fear, but that doesn't mean that there are not gifts to be found and experienced along the way. Take advantage of the knowing that death is coming and then take deep breaths, open your arms, and embrace the living—even as they are dying.

Looking Death in the Eye

The phone rings. Hesitantly, we lift the receiver and await the news we have been dreading, collapsing to the ground when our worst fears come true. *Terminal.* It is a word that creates fear and anguish, often eliciting resentment at the unfairness of the world and questioning why you were chosen to face this battle instead of someone else. Though we would never choose to place this diagnosis on someone else's shoulders, it is human nature to ask "why me?" As the news slowly sinks in, your mind tries to come to terms with the realization that your world has just changed forever. What is often overlooked at this time, is the fact that the lives of our loved ones are forever changed as well. No matter how we choose to look at it, the impact of receiving a terminal diagnosis creates a ripple effect that touches everyone involved in our lives.

Let's take a look at how a terminal diagnosis can greatly impact the lives of those around us. Many people, and it is okay to admit this, are uncomfortable with death and dying—plainly and simply. From the physicians who have difficulty giving us the news, to our friends and even our own family members who avoid conversation and even eye contact, it is easier to divert the subject and walk in circles around the gigantic elephant in the room. What begins to happen almost immediately is the unavoidable journey of grief through knowing that our loved one is going to die and there is nothing we can do about it. Or is there?

Nothing saddens me more than when I visit a patient and/or their family and I hear stories of avoidance. Families question where their support has gone and why friends and family members have stopped calling or dropping by. Caregivers feel overwhelmed with the weight of this new diagnosis, struggling to stay "strong" in the eyes of their loved one while juggling emotions, doctor's appointments, meals, and likely introducing new medications and routines. The patients often crave socialization—needing personal contact, a bedside visit, a story read, a laugh about a good memory, and sometimes just the sweet (but difficult) gift of silence. Having friends and family there and knowing they are present for us is perhaps one of the greatest ways to show our love and support.

So the question often posed is this: Why do we stop doing the things that are the most appreciated and helpful? Death and dying has become almost a "taboo" subject in this day and time. People don't talk about it; they hit the "ignore" button on the phone in order to avoid difficult conversations. Excuses range from, "Well, it's just so hard," to "I don't know what to say." Here is a suggestion: Eveything about death and dying is hard. If it is at all possible, find some inner strength to do the right thing and be present for your loved ones. Upon receiving a terminal diagnosis, our loved ones struggle to find hope and strength in facing their impending death. Some of them fight a valiant fight and teach us lessons that will live forever within us. Let us take the time to look death in the eye and prove to our loved ones and ourselves that "life" and the "quality" of our time left here on earth is worth living!

Weathering the Storm

I distinctly remember sitting in a circle with a group of women who had all recently lost their husbands. It was my first grief support group and I was anxious to see the wondrous miracle of feeling validation and hear the flow of conversation among people who were traveling some very similar paths. What I was not prepared for, however, was being taught a very important lesson; one that was unexpected but never forgotten and often shared by me with others to this day.

At that stage in my life, I had a very immature idea of what grief was and how it was often expressed by others. I was naïve in assuming that grief followed certain stages and in a particular order, never once questioning all I had learned in graduate school or in the many books I had devoured over the years. I confidently started the session by making a statement that changed the way I would look at grief forever. Those of you who know me know of my love for words, symbolism and analogies. In my mind, I thought I had the perfect analogy for grief and decided to share it with those present.

I said to them, "Grief is really, in a lot of ways, like the perfect storm. It resembles the weather in so many ways. At first, there is the constant pouring down of rain and the loud booming of thunder and lightning. Then, after a bit, the rain tapers off into a fine mist and comes to a stop, leading us into our bright and sunny days. But, I warned, there will always be cloudy days and scattered showers ahead, because grief is unpredictable and present in many ways, shapes and forms." Looking around the room, I noticed a lot of head nods and tears, people agreeing with that statement and likening it to what they were currently experiencing. However, as my eyes traversed the group, I noticed there was one lady who was glaring at me with anger and had her hand raised. My heart thudded in my chest as I wondered what on earth I could have said to have upset her in such a fashion.

What she said to me was: "I find your analogy false and misguided for in my grief, I have yet to experience the rain and the thunderstorms. I find myself numb and unable to cry." It was at this moment when I truly realized that not everyone fits into the perfect grief box; even though there are stages of grief, it should not be assumed that we will touch every stage or experience them in any particular order. Many people are not aware of this and try to force themselves into a stage of denial or anger, acceptance or bargaining. They call me and question if they are grieving the right way and point out what a book stated or a certain author wrote. I tell them that grief is constantly evolving, ever changing with our culture and politics, our ideas and our belief systems. I emphasize that stages are just guidelines and not necessarily something we should strive towards, and that our grief will evolve and change on a daily basis as we learn more about ourselves.

Today, I am thankful for having learned that lesson so early on in my career; that one brave lady was able to speak up and share how her experience was different, even though it went against the grain of what others were sharing. I know that many people have similar experiences to hers—delayed responses, the inablity to tap into emotions, feeling stuck or unable to cry. Moments such as these, when I am able to learn from those in the midst of their perfect storm, are moments that stay with me forever and serve as life lessons to share with others. By sharing our grief and our hardships, we can create the glimpses of hope and sunny days that await us just around the corner. We are built to weather many storms, and as my mom always used to assure me, "a little bit of rain won't hurt you."

Turning the Page

For countless numbers of years, people have engaged in the wonderful art of storytelling. Stories are meant to weave together our thoughts and dreams, fantasies and fears. They create an outlet for us to share with others while at the same time providing entertainment and knowledge. What happens when the story we have created for ourselves becomes changed? So many times we find that we are drawn to a main character, their story, their trials, and tribulations. When that character is ripped from the pages and taken out of our lives, it can cause unwanted turmoil and angst. Let's take a look at our own personal stories—their raveling and unraveling and see how grief plays a role.

"In the beginning" is the traditional way a story unfolds—it sets the tone for the genre and the cast of characters soon to follow. As we turn each page, we grow along with the characters, laugh when they engage in humor, grow frustrated when they bumble around and can't seem to find the answers, and cry when tragedy strikes. With a story, there is always a beginning and an end, the pages in between capture the main idea and the message the story is sharing with the reader. However, when we are talking about our own personal grief journey, it should be noted that there is definitely a beginning, but most often, there is not a true ending. Many of you have experienced your own journey and know this to be true—that once we are on this journey, it is a part of us for life. But, what if we were to look at this in a way that would be more pleasing—a journey that never ends, but one that offers the opportunity to grow and create new chapters?

Envision grief in terms of pages or chapters—with each turning of the page or each chapter completed, we find ourselves further along the grief path. Some of those chapters are difficult to focus on and others cause distress and anxiety to the point where we just want to place our bookmark between the pages and put it away for awhile. At other times, we may find ourselves devouring page after page, discovering ourselves several chapters along without even realizing we had consumed so much of the story. And then, there is that moment when we can look back and see that we are already over halfway finished—the end is approaching quickly, with a promised conclusion sure to wrap up everything in a nice little bow (that is, were it simply a story and not our grief narrative).

With grief our stories change; the characters are spun in many different and unexpected directions: lost, lonely and anxiety-laden. Other times we find our characters filled with hope and renewed passion, a yearning for normalcy and unbridled expectations of what is to come. And yet, at other times we struggle with the new story that starts to emerge, the one we never wanted to read or even considered being a part of, for we are there presently and it is ours to own. There will come a time when we realize that our story still has many chapters left; narratives to be told and lived. Remember that our story is ongoing and "The End" is not yet expected. Let us look at our present life and our grief and begin to fill our pages with words, to create our own chapters, and to live each day in its moment, one page at a time. "Once upon a time ...."

Medicine for the Soul

It never ceases to amaze me how often I hear the word "prayer" in connection with those newly bereaved. For many, being in touch with their spiritual side and using the art of prayer is the only safe harbor they have. They tell me over and over again that they don't know what they would do if they didn't have prayer in their lives. And yet, for others, prayer is the farthest thing from their minds—they are lost and confused, beaten and battered by the waves of grief. As a child, I remember finding myself in prayer during church, reciting the words along with others, wondering about God and how He could possibly hear and answer the wishes of so many. I would feel guilty because I often used prayer just when I wanted something. For example, "Dear God, please let me make an 'A' on my History test" or "Dear God, it would be really great if I could make the All-Star team." It wasn't until I was much older that prayer took on a new meaning for me. I began to understand the "power of prayer" and how it could not only influence my life, but also the lives of others.

Not long ago, a gentleman was talking about the hardships he had been facing since his mother died. He spoke about his faith and his prayers, sharing with us a message that rang loud and clear. After his mom died, he had asked God to give him a sign that she was okay and that she was in His loving hands in the heaven in which he so strongly believed. He shared, "At first I didn't think God was listening because He wouldn't show me a sign. I felt abandoned and lost in my grief. But suddenly I realized that if God gave me a sign, then I would greedily ask for another one, and then another one—never satisfied and always seeking more. It was only then that I knew everything was going to be okay and that by not answering me, He had spoken very loudly and shown me the way." All I could do in this moment was listen and absorb the grace he shared. The words left a lasting impact on me.

I once met with a woman who was also newly bereaved. Her friends and family had been providing love and support and constantly asked what they could do to help her along her grief journey. She simply stated, "Pray for me that I will find the strength to get through this." She turned away from them to walk down the hall and entering her bedroom she noticed a bracelet on the floor. She picked it up, never having seen it before, and not knowing where it had come from. She looked at the word that was etched upon it—"strength." Placing the band around her wrist, she smiled knowing that God had "just answered her prayer."

Sometimes, when the weight of our sadness is too much to bear, I think of stories such as these and know that we are often given messages from above just when we need them the most. I try to be alert to these "gifts" because if we are unwilling to see them, we could miss the opportunity to experience their wonder and the healing they might offer. However, I must admit that these "gifts" are often easy to miss when our eyes are clouded with grief. Keep in mind that just like flipping a switch, there will be a time in your journey when your eyes will be unexpectedly opened, and it will be up to you to embrace what is given. At the time, you may not be ready to see what is being offered, but that is the glory of life, because I choose to believe that we will be given plenty of other opportunities. Just like taking medicine, the message may be unpleasant in the moment, but the medicine will begin to work its power and the true healing can begin. Prayer may not be the answer to everything, however, just like taking medicine, if you add a little sugar, it might just help everything go down a little bit easier. Amen.

Messages From Above

Have you ever heard of receiving pennies from heaven? Or what about dimes on the doorstep or beautiful butterflies perched outside our window? If you have, you might smile and place a hand over your heart at a particular memory or experience that you are certain was an "after-death message" from your loved one. Over the years, I have listened in absolute wonder to stories shared from families about signs our loved ones have given to us from beyond—and I truly believe that if we are open to signs, we are much more likely to experience them. Sure, there are those who are unwilling to entertain such thoughts and there are others who are constantly looking for some kind of sign. The truth of the matter is that if we pay close attention to the world around us, there are many gifts that are given freely if we are only open to seeing them.

I have been meeting with a dear, sweet lady who has been on her grief journey for almost nine months. Like most of us, she has her good days and her difficult ones. She firmly believes that her departed husband has placed people in her life to help guide her along this difficult journey, her "angels sent from heaven": a random person working out next to her on a treadmill who has also lost a husband, a person filling a prescription at a local pharmacy who shared about her loss, a lady she ran into at a support group who needed someone to talk to about the death of her husband, etc. When I would arrive for our sessions, she was often eager to share with me a story about a "new message" that she had received—one that lifted her up on her darkest day and propelled her forward even though she lacked the motivation.

On one particular day, she shared with me about a song that she heard on the radio entitled "What Becomes of the Brokenhearted," a great song from the 1960s by Jimmy Ruffin. When listening to the words, they seemed to wrap around her and describe perfectly the feelings she had been having since the death of her husband. And, then something glorious happened; she remembered that her husband used to love to make CDs of his favorite music. She went on a mission looking for his collection and almost immediately discovered the CD with that very song. Again, she felt like her husband was speaking to her and enveloping her in his spiritual self, providing unseen but heartfelt comfort.

When I looked at the CD cover that she so proudly showed me, I was struck by the obvious "signs from above" that were displayed on that cover. In his scratchy handwriting, the favorites he had listed on that CD went as follows: "What Becomes of the Brokenhearted," "The Tracks of My Tears," "Rescue Me," "People Get Ready," "Where Did Our Love Go?," "My Girl," "Dancing in the Streets," and "Back in my Arms Again." As I pointed out the songs listed, in that particular order, her eyes lit up with delight. Out of all the CDs he had in his study, this simple collection from 1964-1967 that he had compiled years ago, seemed to be chosen just for her. What greater moment than to witness the surge of absolute joy and exultation—her hands fisted around that yellow cover, her eyes twinkling with the knowledge that her husband had indeed picked out this selection just for her because maybe, just maybe, he knew she would need to listen to those words one day. Now, whether it was a message from beyond the grave or not, she is choosing to believe that he has sent her yet another "sign from above." As I left her home, I turned on my car radio and heard the song "Don't Stop Believing" by Journey. After the morning I had just had, I could only smile, receiving that message loud and clear, and reached down to turn up the volume.

Grief: The Spiritual Side of Healing

Often, when I am making visits or phone calls to the newly bereaved, the topic of spirituality comes up. For some, the response is instant for their faith is rock solid and their belief system tends to be the main thing that is "getting them through." However, for others, death can be faith shaking and instead of being rock solid, everything that they thought they knew or believed has been rattled to its very core. Responses I have heard can be anything from, "The Lord is carrying me through" to "The Lord has abandoned me." And, on top of everything else, church communities are either very supportive or surprisingly absent—yet another issue that is sure to influence the way in which we grieve.

As I mentioned in a previous column, it is important that we work on healing not just our physical and emotional selves, but our spiritual selves as well. What exactly does that mean, especially if one does not belong to a particular church or religious group? And, how does one go about healing? What if we are long-standing members of a particular church, but we are unsure if that is the place we still need to be?

It never surprises me when people choose to talk about the difficulties of going back to church after a loved one dies, especially if it is a spouse that they have shared countless numbers of memories together with in that sanctuary. The many rituals of Sunday mornings become difficult in our grief—the selection of our church clothes, the emptiness of the pew (the one on which you had always sat next to each other hand in hand), the facing of our friends who are either hesitant to speak because they don't wish to make us sad, or who openly display pity and rush to hug us which often causes tears and sadness to erupt—a reaction we had simply hoped to avoid. I also hear them talk about the emptiness they feel as something shifts inside of them and with sudden clarity they realize that their souls are no longer being fed. There is often guilt expressed because they feel as though they should stay loyal to a church that has been a part of their lives for so long, however the loneliness is too hard to bear and propels them inside the doors of another church, trying to find what it is that is missing, and seeking enlightenment and healing.

To practice spiritual self-care is an essential part of the journey for some, and it often gives us the courage to find meaning in our continuing lives. I say this so that you know that you have permission to search and explore, that it is okay to initiate an absence from your regular church or from your chosen religion, while you take the time to seek what it is that your heart needs. And, likewise, it is okay to rely on your faith and your belief system to see you through some of the most difficult aspects of your journey. Remember that everyone's needs and the way in which they grieve are unique, so we must respect the fact that one person's spiritual healing may look completely different from someone else's.

I truly believe that balance is the key that will unlock our deepest and darkest hurts. If we are able to take care of our physical bodies, share our feelings and emotions in a healthy manner and examine where we stand spiritually, it is bound to go a long way toward our overall healing. Keep in mind that our spirituality is ours and ours alone—it is up to us to build it up, to shut it down, or to find comfort in the familiarity of where we have always been. Again, if we are open to listening to and receiving messages, there are bound to be countless examples of insight that will nurture us through this most difficult time.

Helen Keller, a blind woman who was able to "see" more than most due to her incredible insight and the value she placed on growth and understanding stated, "The only way to the other side is through." Let us take the time to examine where we are in our journey, and then choose the path that will carry us forward in our quest for finding and accepting inner peace.

Solitude and Community

"We bereaved are not alone. We belong to the largest company in all the world—the company of those who have known suffering."

– Helen Keller

Anger Danger

If we are being honest, we have all experienced anger in its purest form at one time or another. It can be raw, wild, and so out of control at times that it can be difficult to rein in, often creating moments that we are later ashamed of and would like to have back. Anger is natural. Anger is part of a rainbow of emotions. It can be fleeting or can linger inside, stirring up all kinds of negativity, guilt and all around "just no good" thoughts. When it arises, it is important to take notice of what may have triggered this response and then get down to the dirty work of figuring out the underlying issues that may have brought about this latest explosion.

Everyone has heard about "road rage." Not only have I heard about it, but for a while, I was the *queen* of road rage and everyone who pulled out in front of me or drove slowly in the fast lane would receive an earful of unbridled anger, oftentimes filled with (gulp) expletives and mad pounding on the steering wheel. It wasn't until my daughter, probably about nine at the time and wise beyond her years, innocently said to me after one of these episodes, "Mom, why do you yell at them? They can't hear you and all you're doing is hurting your car." For a moment, I wanted to argue with her about the inconsiderate person that made me slow down when I was in a hurry and how it was their fault that I was so upset, but then I realized that she was absolutely right. What was the point?

The point was that I had been allowing anger to build inside of me. I let it fester and boil just below the surface and it was starting to eat me alive. Being a grief counselor allows me to take on the weight of everyone's sadness and it is a weight that I willingly carry, however, it is also imperative that I find ways to disperse some of that sadness in ways that are healthy and healing for me. Honestly, I decided I needed to walk the walk a little bit better than I had been doing and I needed to start right away. Since that moment, there have still been days in which the anger erupts and I feel ashamed that I allowed it to reach that point. I recognize that it is not something that I need to ignore and I immediately start working on discovering inner peace and healing.

When we are grieving, it is easy to become caught up in anger; anger that our loved one has died; anger that our dreams have been shattered; anger that our friendships have changed or that maybe someone who was once always present is no longer as available. Anger can take on many forms and it can quickly become the ruler of our unhappiness and discontent. What I always remind people of is the simple fact that anger can be a "healthy" emotion. It can. Anger helps us to identify the depths of our feelings and allows us to examine the hardcore sadness, pain and discontent that lies within. It can be a friend or a foe but we must be honest with ourselves and try to accept the message it is trying to convey.

With anger oftentimes comes tears. And, that makes us even more angry because we don't like to cry. Losing a loved one can produce an anger that is unfamiliar because anger is a secondary emotion to the sadness that we now feel. Our loss fuels our negative feelings and can confuse us because it is not in our nature to feel such intense emotions. Give yourself permission to feel everything, every single emotion good or bad, during this difficult time. There are lessons there, and by experiencing them, acknowledging them and processing our grief, we can only become stronger for having faced them.

Body Grief: Signs and Symptoms

We have all experienced, at one time or another, an obvious sign of stress or anxiety—whether it is stomachache, headache, muscle tension, or other physical symptom. It frustrates us because it appears to be out of our control, a natural response to something that makes us feel uneasy or afraid. For example, going to the dentist (with my humble apologies to the dental field), as my appointment draws closer, my body betrays me and my anxiety about going surfaces in many unpleasant ways. It is not rational to find myself so worked up over a simple cleaning, but it is what it is, and for my entire life I have had to deal with it. Others find it difficult to speak in front of a crowd or perform on stage, thus creating the familiar phrase "stage fright," leaving us feeling immobile and sometimes paralyzed by our fear.

After we have experienced the traumatic death of a loved one, grief takes on many different forms—some that we are expecting and others that create additional worries or concerns. What is important to remember is that grief affects us both emotionally and physically. In general, individuals tend to pay closer attention to the emotions they are feeling and spend less time on how the physical body responds. And yet, the two are intertwined—one affects the other and both need to be addressed for optimal healing.

It is very important during our time of mourning to pay close attention to what our body is trying to tell us. Sometimes we find ourselves too busy to notice some warning signs, and other times we choose to ignore them because our emotional hurt has become the primary focus. No one knows our body better than we do and when our body starts to scream and shout, it is time to listen. Just because we are grieving, we mustn't overlook these signs. It is necessary to take a moment and pay attention to what our body needs. So, what *does* our body need and how does it express itself?

Some of the most common physical symptoms experienced by the grieving are: exhaustion, stomach distress, poor or excessive appetite, severe headaches, tingling and numbness in the face or arms, chest pain, body aches and sleep disturbance. Many people share that they feel like they are having a "heart attack" because the symptoms they are experiencing mimic a cardiac event. Physicians are often consulted and we are told it is more likely a panic or anxiety attack" and that our bodies are stressed and we need more rest. This can be both frightening and confusing when it occurs because we are convinced that we are dying and no one is listening to us. But then, the symptoms start to fade and we realize how truly sensitive our bodies are to stress and trauma.

Unfortunately with grief, we can't take a magic pill and make all the hurt and unpleasant feelings go away. However, we can do simple things to maintain our bodies to ensure that we are taking care of ourselves while we are on our grief journey. Some of the ways we can do this are: drink plenty of water (this hydrates us and gives us energy to combat our daily obstacles), rest when able, find ways to express feelings, keep doctor's appointments or schedule one if needed, eat healthy and try to incorporate some exercise into your daily routine. Remember that our aches and pains are giving us notice that we need to take care of ourselves in order to allow optimal healing. And lastly, true healing only comes through nourishing the mind, the body, *and* the soul.

No Such Thing as "Letting Go"

Time and time again, I find myself holding the hand of someone who is feeling intense anguish over the death of a loved one. I watch as friends and family members gather around and encourage each other to say "goodbye" so that they can have some "closure" and "move on." I don't know about you, but every time I hear those words, I cringe and feel like my insides will burst. Why should we have to tell our loved ones a final goodbye? Is there some unwritten rule stating that since they are no longer physically present with us that we have to erase them from our memory? Are we supposed to snap our fingers and make things magically go away because it is essential that we have some closure? Where did that word even come from, and why is it so important to others that we achieve it?

Essentially, what I find myself doing is engaging in a gentle redirecting of the frame of mind. When people tell me they have to "let go" of their loved one, I simply challenge them with a one question—"Why?" Why do we have to close them out of our lives? Why do we have to go through their belongings as soon as possible and give them away? Why do we have to tell them goodbye? I let them know that the years we spent loving them have been, and always will be, a part of our lives and that we never, ever have to let go of those things. It is true that at some point in our grief journey, we start to adapt to the loss and change does occur. We do find a sense of belonging in what is known as our "new normal," but that doesn't mean we have closed the door on all of those memories we created, to be sent away forever with a forced "goodbye."

It should be stressed that our loved ones continue along our grief journey with us—ever present and ever painful. By talking about them, sharing memories and stories, we are basically keeping them alive and a part of our hearts forever. We do not need to close them out or place them on the shelf like a long lost book that was once so dear to us. The lives of our loved ones should be lived and cherished. We should let our friends and family know that we have no intention of "closing" them out of our lives; neither should we have to "let them go." They should understand that the brilliant scar on our hearts, the pain from their loss is evident in our daily lives. We choose to live our grief journey with them spiritually present, alongside us, every single step of the way. Instead of saying "goodbye" we are choosing instead to say "hello" to a new day with them guiding us along our grief journey.

Shakespeare said it best when he wrote, "Parting is such sweet sorrow." Death creates a melancholy unlike anything we have ever known, and when the physical "parting" does occur, there is indeed sorrow. However, over time, that sorrow can develop into a sweetness that satisfies the intense desire to "hold on" to our loved one's memories and never "let them go."

Sowing the Seeds of Sorrow

As the time change moved our clocks forward this week, sending us into the early beginnings of spring, I am reminded of new life. All around us, birds have emerged from their nests, their songs filling the air; trees are starting to gather new buds and display bursts of green; and everywhere you look, shoots are bursting from the ground with vibrant displays of color and beauty. Spring is definitely a time of reawakening; a time when we are shaking off the habits of deep slumber, bitter cold, and dreary rain. Our eyes are open to the wonders of all the changes around us, but sometimes we feel the bitterness that comes about when we have lost a loved one, and spring is simply a reminder of all that we have lost—a pill that is often difficult to swallow.

Most gardeners will tell you that spring is the time for planting. With all the recent rains and the last of the winter cold waving us a forlorn goodbye, the ground is ripe for receiving flowers, shrubs, and trees. Wouldn't it be wonderful to look at our grief journey and think about it as a small seed—a seed that we have planted and are about to watch grow? Think of yourself as the gardener who has taken careful measure of the weather, the time of year, and has carefully selected the life we would like to now nurture and bring forth. Grief is our tiny seed. When born, it remains locked away inside its shell, protected and dark within its binding husk. Placed in the ground, it is then surrounded by nourishment—the earth's nutrient dirt, fertilizers, and natural surroundings. Over time, the rain contributes to the growth process, seeping down into the ground and enveloping the seed. Soon, the seed gives way to the tiniest of cracks and the first shoot begins to emerge, seeking light through the darkness.

How wonderful is the day that we notice movement! The dirt shifts and after inspecting closely, we see the smallest bit of green striving to make it out of the confines of its previous home. We atr amazed as each day that stalk grows stronger and taller—impervious to everything around it, determined to soak up the light of the sun. Think about grief in this manner: sometimes our planted seed takes longer to emerge from its casing, seeming determined to stay locked up tight, where it feels safe and warm. But then one day, it decides to stretch, and that crack opens, letting in a little bit of light—the light that had seemed to be missing for so long. Encouraged by that light, we shuck off the remaining shell of our casing and reach toward the warmth of the sun. As we break the surface, we are reminded that we are still alive and have just experienced growth in our grief journey.

Everyone's tiny seed along the grief path is different and unique. Some choose to stay dormant for an entire year and only emerge after much time has passed, gathering the strength they need to make the journey upwards. Others are more determined and force themselves out of their shell, oftentimes before they are really ready, which may cause challenges that can be hard to overcome. And then, there are those who wallow in the dark, absorb all of their surroundings and gather the strength they need to make their journey upwards. The growth process is scientific and takes a lot of factors into account; and so, too, is the grief journey. When thinking about your seed and the growth you have experienced thus far, be mindful that there will always be some sunny days, but rain is what truly makes the flowers grow.

Spelling Out Our Grief

With all of the advances in technology, the act of human touch has all but disappeared. Where once we took the time to hand write a letter, we now email or send text messages using our computers and phones. People are no longer used to calling others and hearing a voice on the other end because we are so focused on running from here to there and "don't have the time" for conversation. As a grief counselor, I spend a lot of time with the older generation—you know, the ones born in the 20s and 30s—the ones who suffered through the Great Depression and understood what family and being neighborly meant. Listening to them share their heartache about lost communication and the cold, sterile sound of a text message notification made me think about all that has been lost. What can we do about it?

Sitting with a ninety-three-year-old who is slowly dying from a lung disease, I listen to her share the importance of human contact. She has to pause every few words due to her inability to breathe while the oxygen mask she wears hisses in its attempt to provide her with the nourishment she desperately needs. In her storytelling, she mentioned a dear friend that she had lost contact with over ten years ago. Once the friend knew that her health was failing, she made a point to come and visit her. The time they spent reconnecting was enough to give her energy for days and the smile on her face to have had that time with her was telling. In her wisdom, she knew that any visit could probably be her last and made it a point to enjoy each moment as it was presented. Like the good old days, they sat across from each other and played *Scrabble*. You know, the original word game that made us use our brains and to race to the dictionary to prove that our triple word score was truly a word?

As she spoke, a grief trigger hit me out of nowhere—surprising me in its intensity. I could see myself in my younger years, somewhere between the ages of seven and ten, pigtails and face full of freckles, sitting across from my grandfather—the game of *Scrabble* laid out before us. I could see his handwriting on an old pad with scores scribbled upon it and smell the wood tiles as I pulled open the drawstring of the bag that held them. Those moments were special to me—my time with my grandfather. It didn't matter if the word was D-O-G or A-P-P-L-E, he praised my intellect and the ability to form words—a passion of his—and he was proud of me. It's not that I loved the game so much, instead it was the need for that kind of affection. I craved his positive reinforcement and encouragement. My love of words and the forming of ideas grew each year as we played, and after he died, I was gifted with that wonderful *Scrabble* board (the one in the small maroon box with wooden tile holders)—a symbol of love, relationships, and nourishment for my soul. Yes, I have the brand new version made of reinforced plastic that spins around so it is easier for everyone to see the board, and I also own the travel pocket-size edition so you can *"Scrabble"* on the go. But none of those, as fancy as they are, can ever replace the one that evokes such strong and compelling memories of the man I lost over twenty years ago.

By listening to this special ninety-three-year-old lady, I received the gift of "remembering." She sent me down memory lane and I was momentarily lost in the feelings and emotions that were as clear as if they had just happened yesterday. Because I had taken the time to be present for her and to listen, and because human contact is so important, especially when you are examining the end of your life and know your time is limited, we were both able to receive comfort. When we are preparing for our own death, or when we are remembering the death of a special loved one, the multitude of feelings can be overwhelming. The phrase "rest a spell" ran through my mind as I watched her struggle to breathe, but also recognized that she didn't want me to leave her side. Words, games, listening, the act of human touch—all of these things are vital and should not be avoided. Whether we are preparing for death or remembering, the compassion we need to demonstrate to others shouldn't have to be "spelled out." Think about your role today—draw a tile, roll the dice, formulate what you wish to say and then take your turn. Only by making an effort in the game of life can we truly become a W-I-N-N-E-R.

The Sound of Silence

No matter how many times it is spoken to me, it seems to cut to the bone when I hear about how quiet grief can be to some individuals experiencing loss. Never in my wildest dreams did I ever envision that grief would be quiet. Instead, I pictured loud outbursts of sadness—crying, anger, the hustle and bustle of settling legal affairs and sorting through of countless mounds of paperwork. I expected piercing screams, the mournful wailing of loss, and maybe even the crude punching of fists against immovable walls. Loud. Sometimes grief is so loud that it becomes uncomfortable for both the person displaying it and for those in attendance. Not once did I stop to consider that grief can also be quiet. That silence, in actuality, is loud.

Sitting on the veranda of a beautiful historic home, watching the porch swing in the fall breeze, I listen as I am told about the power of silence; how it grabs ahold of people and squeezes until they are forced to pay attention. When everything is quiet, you can literally hear the memories of all the days gone by. When everything is quiet, you can sense the former laughter as it dances around you, bringing both comfort and a deep resounding pain. Only when everything is quiet can we take the time for reflection and examine the person within us that has been changed forever.

For most of us, the settling in of nighttime is the most quiet. But, because it is quiet, it is also the loudest. How can that be? Though the body rests, the mind is still active, processing memories and recalling times spent together. We are inundated with feelings of loss so painful that at times we try our hardest to stay busy making noise, essentially avoiding the silence that waits to embrace us. Many who are on their grief journey simply cannot welcome the silence—it hurts way too much. However, the truth of the matter is that the silence remains because the person who is now absent, at least for now, has taken with them the life that created your sound. We are oblivious to the world around us even though the world is still active. We enshroud ourselves in the quiet, in the silence, with hopes of avoiding the sheer scream of death.

Simon and Garfunkel penned one of the greatest songs of all time and the lyrics speak to the path on which mourners often find themselves walking. The words are: "People talking without speaking; People hearing without listening; hear my words that I might teach you; Take my arms that I might reach you." Those words define the enigma of silence in so many ways. And unfortunately, something that is also very evident is that silence is like a cancer ... it grows. It grows and grows until it is out of our control and we may need others to tap into our quietude to remind us that there is indeed life outside of our protective cocoon. Today, take some time to contemplate how grief can be quiet and it can be loud, and let us work together through the "sound of silence."

An Unwanted Journey

Repeatedly, I speak to the newly bereaved about their grief, often referring to this new stage in their life as their "grief journey." To me, it symbolizes that grief is a destination—that it is a quest of rediscovery and a redefinition of the life that we once knew but must find a way to live once again. At a recent grief support group, one of the members stated, "You always talk about this as being a journey, but what is really difficult for me is that I am always wondering, a journey to where?"

As the heads nodded around the room, it became apparent to me that even though each individual's grief is unique, it also holds a common factor—a sense that there is a collective loss of direction. Each of them was able to verbalize that they understood that grief was a passage, a trip that was never ending. Each spoke of times and places, shared memories and experiences, and yet, all seemed unclear of their destination. What I told them was this: Grief is truly a journey that no one wants to be on. That is a fact. However, with life comes death, and we are all going to experience the gut-wrenching heartache of loss at some point in our lives. Once this happens, there is simply no set time limit on, or clear ending to, our grief. In fact, what happens is that we begin to engage in a life that has altered our way of living. Some people describe this as the "new normal." However, that is not really a phrase that resonates with me because it seems to somehow discount the loss of the life we had—that we must accept our losses and move on. Though there is some truth to the statement that moving on is a part of our journey, when we reach that point and how we get there is a different matter entirely.

What is important to remember when talking about our journey is that it is ever changing. Some days are easier than others and there are sure to be moments when we emphatically state that we simply cannot go on and would rather join our loved ones in death. Please note that these are normal reactions. Pain is hard and only by experiencing these things can we grow and move forward. Think of a puzzle and imagine trying to put that puzzle together without seeing the picture on the box. All you have in front of you is a pile of pieces in complete disarray with no clear understanding of where to begin. Grief is like that in the beginning, but once we start fitting some pieces together, the picture becomes clearer and we begin to see the pieces of the life we are putting back together. However, just like a puzzle that has sat in the closet for a few years, or was purchased at a yard sale, there may be a few pieces missing. If this has ever happened to you, you know the frustration and anxiety that develops when you see that you cannot complete the puzzle. Again, this describes our grief because once we lose someone so dear and beloved to us, we simply cannot pick up all the pieces and put them back together again. There will always be something missing and the pain in our hearts reminds us how much this is true.

Those who know me know that I always like to close each group or support session with a focus on positive news. Though the grief journey is truly an unwanted experience in our lives, I try to help those who are on it to focus on the things they have learned about themselves by having faced it. Watching their growth and witnessing them rediscover themselves is a reward like no other. For me, it is well worth the cost of the ticket to assist those who are traveling in my direction.

Communicating With Others Can Be a Tall Task

Too many times, people who are newly bereaved approach me to say that they are simply overwhelmed by the number of phone calls and visits that people are making to offer support. They describe refrigerators and freezers full of food. They are now faced with the task of finding something to do with the plethora of casseroles on hand, or tracking down the owner of a *Pyrex* container or *Tupperware* bowl. Because death and loss can be an uncomfortable subject, those who wish to offer comfort often feel unsure as to what they can say or do to be helpful. In the south, the most common tactic we use is to parade food in for the family so we can be assured that they are eating and taking care of themselves. It makes us feel good to be able to "do something," and so after this buffet of good eats is partaken of, we tend to move along and forget that our role for those who are bereaved should include more than simply filling up their belly. What else can we do?

Part of the role of caregiver/supporter should be about communicating to our loved one that we are present and available for *whatever* they need. In saying this, we need to be accountable and actually follow through with this action and not assume that they will call us "*if* they need us." Why is this important? Because grief can be debilitating—causing us to feel lost and confused. At times, we cannot even track what day it is or what we need to be doing, let alone think clearly enough to know what to ask for from friends and family members. For those with limited support, a thoughtful card, an invitation to dinner, or a social outing can be helpful. However, there are those who are overwhelmed by all the invitations and grow frustrated by everyone's "helpfulness." They just want to be left alone.

A wise man once shared with me that, "Everyone keeps telling me I need to do this and I need to do that. Why can't they see that I need some time to be alone—to simply 'be' with the memories of my wife and find some time to heal?" What I told him, and what I think can be very advantageous for those grieving and for those supporting them is this: "People are looking for cues from you. Tell them what it is that you need and don't worry about whether or not the request is too much or not enough. Be aware that what you might need today may become just the opposite tomorrow, because that is the way grief works." For example, if you were to attend a social gathering, you may have let people know that it is too hard for everyone to come up to you and ask how you are doing. You may have instructed them to just avoid the topic of your loss and enjoy the occasion. However, later, back at home, you may feel devastated that "nobody cared enough to approach you and ask how you were doing." That is why communication is so important. Talking about our feelings, our hurt, and loss is difficult enough. Learning how to reach out to others and ask for help can be just as foreign. Human nature allows us to be "helpful" and "kind to others," but it is rare when we choose to ask for help—ever determined to handle things on our own.

Today, remember that grief is better shared than carried alone. Beyond the hugs, cards, and well wishes, let us use our words to reach into the hearts of those who are hurting and communicate to them that we are here in whatever capacity we are needed—now and forever.

Loss Comes in Many Disguises

I once asked teenagers to take a mask and decorate the outside to demonstrate what they wanted others to see about their feelings after the death of their loved ones. The second part of the task was for them to turn over the mask and decorate the inside to demonstrate what thoughts and feelings they were holding onto on the inside—away from others. As you can guess, the inside was filled with hurt and pain, sadness and loss. The outside tended to display a "happy" face or words of indifference—making a clear statement that "all was well"—an attempt to keep their feelings hidden away from those who would look to pick apart their grief.

In today's society, the strange notion that we have to keep our feelings hidden continues to rear its ugly head. People discuss how difficult it is to let their guard down and share with others that their hurt is paralyzing, fearful that they will be judged as having the lack of strength or fortitude to make it through such a difficult time. No where was this more apparent than when a woman shared with me that her friend had made the flippant comment, "I can't wait until the old you comes back." Not only was this extremely hurtful, but the anger that poured out was fierce and strong in her response. "Doesn't she know that the *old* me is gone? How can I ever be the same after my husband has died? His death has changed me *forever*." Kudos to her for recognizing that her friend's expectations of her were unrealistic and for confronting the statement for what it was—a remark made by someone who "hasn't been there."

Too often I witness, or participate in, discussions where people have felt judged for grieving. Think about that for a moment. People are judged for openly being sad about the loss of their loved one. Most of us shake our heads in disbelief and wonder how people can be so cruel. We wonder how a world can exist where assumptions are made and friendships lost simply because we have become inconvenienced by someone's grief. The truth of the matter is that this happens more often than you know, and it is an issue that needs to be addressed, examined, dissected, and then given its proper platform. Grieving is a right. It is also a part of life in which we need for others to be supportive and understanding—the rock or the anchor that keeps us grounded—waiting for the time when we are ready to accept the help they are offering. Not everyone is accepting of support and sometimes this can cause friendships to go awry because they don't understand what we need or how to be present. But, to assume that we know how they feel or to wait for them to "get back to normal" is an injustice to them that speaks louder than words.

As I mentioned before, people don't generally like to share their feelings or open up to others about how grief changes them. However, what they do often share with me is the additional hurt and loss they feel when they are expected to grieve a certain way—and when they don't, when their loss propels them in a direction that is uncomfortable for others—they are shunned, left out of social gatherings or even abandoned completely by those they once considered friends and family. Additional losses such as these can impact the grief journey in a severe way often causing feelings of worthlessness and confusion. The grieving tend to literally drown in the sadness they feel because the death of their loved one is already difficult to bear, then the perceived loss of their support system is just too much.

In closing, remember that grief does not fit into a box. As human beings, we need to recognize that not everyone grieves the same. When we choose to ignore the hurt that others feel; fail to realize that their lives have changed forever; or expect them to become someone they no longer know or understand—we validate for them that their mask needs to stay firmly planted on the "happy side." Wouldn't it be wonderful if we could reach the point in our being present for others where we acknowledge that death creates permanent changes? In doing so, we invite the grieving to remove the mask they have felt was needed, to tap into their hidden grief, and share with us their true selves.

Endings and Beginnings

"I will not say: do not weep; for not all tears are an evil."

– J.R.R. Tolkien

Jenny Filush-Glaze | 59

Why Hospice?

I will never forget the conversation I had with a gentleman a few years ago. It has stuck with me and is still the motivation for the due diligence I take in educating our community on anything and everything about "hospice." This man, while on his grief journey, was sharing with me about all the wonderful support he had received during the forty-eight hours in which hospice took care of his mother. He stated many times how relieved he was to know that he was not alone, and that he would never have been able to make it through some of those difficult times without having received specialized care. Overall, he was saddened and exhausted by the death of his mother, yet he still felt gratitude for the presence of hospice. There was one thing that was causing him extreme guilt and anguish, however, and so he asked "Why didn't anyone refer my mother sooner?"

Over the years, I have come to realize that there are many misconceptions of what the word "hospice" actually means. Many view it as signifying the "end of life" that death is "imminent" and it becomes a word that is feared and widely misunderstood. What I know in my heart is that "hospice" isn't a place but is instead a philosophy of care that focuses on comfort, quality of life, and the ability to provide support services for both the patient and their family. Many bypass the offer of hospice because they believe it is a "last resort" measure only to be used in the final few days or hours of life. The reality is that hospice is at least a six-month benefit for those diagnosed with a terminal illness and can provide anything from twenty-four hour RN care, spiritual and bereavement support, certified nursing assistants, social work services, and even volunteers.

As the gentleman stated, he felt like his mother and his family could have benefitted from receiving an earlier referral and was agonizing over what he could have done differently to advocate for his mother. He made sure to point out that he might have made some different decisions in his mother's care had he known what was available and what kind of support would be provided. He mused, "How many other families are missing out on the benefits of hospice simply because they were not aware of when it can be offered and how it can be helpful?" Though it is certain that there are many families facing similar situations, I was unable to give him a definitive answer. Instead, we talked about the advances of medicine and how society as a whole tends to focus on the "fixing and healing" of our loved ones, versus the palliative care and philosophy of hospice, which looks instead at quality of life and comfort measures.

Even though I work for a hospice organization, I have been in situations with my own family members where I wondered why a referral hadn't been made sooner. I recognize that the word "hospice" tends to interfere with our "hope" and our desire for our loved ones to get better and to live longer. If you mention "hospice," sometimes there is anger and desperation expressed, along with the emphatic statement of "I'm not giving up." I *get* it. There has always been a really fine line between what is perceived as "throwing in the towel" and "acknowledging that quality of life is being impacted by countless amounts of treatments and hospital stays." The only recommendation I have is that you begin looking into services that are available once a terminal diagnosis is made; talk with your loved one about their wishes; and formulate a plan with your physician (this is far from giving up).

Sometimes, our desperation to hold on to our loved ones impacts our decision making and we are left trying to cope the best that we know how with friends and family, but with very limited resources. Think of "hospice" as an opportunity to share with others the privileged journey of caring for you and your loved one. Even in hospice, the focus is on "LIVING" and not on "DYING," so feel free to ask questions and gather information on how a benefit such as this could be helpful to you and your family. Yes, hospice coming into your life does mean that time is limited, but that doesn't have to mean hours, days, weeks or months. Choosing hospice is actually a gift of time given to you and your family so that you may be present for them while others are present for you.

The Last Conversation

I want to start this column by giving kudos to our local libraries for taking the initiative to order and place on the shelves some very informative reading for our community. Recently, I have all but devoured books that tackle the difficult subjects of end-of-life care and "dying well." The one that I just finished was written by a hospitalist who focused on the importance of having that last conversation with our family and physicians about how we want to spend the last days of our life. He stated that after many interviews, over ninety-eight percent of people reported that they would like to die at home with their family and friends, but that in reality, less than twenty-three percent are actually able to do so. The question that kept racing through his mind was, "Where are we failing in our healthcare system, and how can we better take care of our patients at the end of their lies?"

Time and time again, I find myself having serious discussions with patients and their families about end-of-life care. For many, just the word "hospice" creates a sense of fear and anxiety and so people, including doctors, tend to tiptoe around the subject in order to avoid any difficult conversations. In reality, studies show that if we are having conversations about our end-of-life care early enough, and if our physicians are on board, hospice care can actually extend our lives. How is this possible? The theory is that we are then able to be content with our decision and are more focused on being comfortable, surrounded by our family and friends. This does not mean that we have given up or that we are forfeiting our life—rather, we are having an honest conversation with ourselves that we are intent on "dying well." What *exactly* does this mean?

Examples given in his book show that families are often unaware of their loved one's end of life wishes. Because of this, when we reach the point where treatments no longer work and our hospital stays are becoming more and more frequent, we are quickly approaching a time in which our window of making good, sound decisions is disappearing. You may have heard of Living Wills or Advance Directives but thought to yourself that you will examine them later in life, or "when you need it." Unfortunately, life is unpredictable and it can suddenly be too late for those conversations we "meant to have," thus placing ourselves in situations where we have to make decisions that are difficult because we are unaware of our loved one's wants and wishes.

One of the blessings I received at an early age was my dad approaching me to have that "last conversation." At the time, I wanted to brush him off and change the subject because I didn't want to think about it or even entertain the thought that one day he might need me to help make a very important decision about his health care. But, I listened, paid attention, and am content in knowing that I have all the information I will need if and when the occasion arises that I am called upon to make a decision. I recall sitting, as a child, at the kitchen table watching my grandfather do the same thing with my dad. Though it unsettled me at the time, I was touched by the moment and knew in my heart that the conversation had given my grandfather peace of mind and heart.

I want to encourage you to have those conversations with your family and with your physician. Do some research and make your intentions and wishes clear so that everyone is on the same page. Having this discussion can be uncomfortable and difficult, but what a blessing it will be at the end of life when everyone is clear about our dying wishes. It is truly heartbreaking to watch a family struggle as they try to make a decision when feelings are raw and uncertain. Make the time to sit down and have that conversation today—it might just be the best gift you will ever give to your family. Giving the gift of clarity means that in the end, we are able to "die well."

As Death Approaches

I sit silently in the corner of the room and wait. Throughout the day, I am amazed at the numbers of people that come in and out of this small space. Some stay awhile while others are quick to come in, do their job, check vitals and leave. I watch as the loving, caring wife sits bedside and her range of emotions throughout the day baffles me, comforts me and at times, soothes me. I know that she is aware of her husband's impending death because I can feel it seeping out of her every pore. Her prayers reverberate around the room, making my ears perk up in order to catch every last word. And, I sigh deeply knowing that my job is to sit and observe—my time to act, to perform my duty has not yet arrived.

For days now, I have hovered nearby and only briefly have I caught glimpses of the soul within the man lying in the bed. At times, his eyes will flutter open and he will catch a glimpse of me. His hands, trembling and weak, appear to reach out to touch me and yet no one else can sense that I am present. His smile lights up the bright blue of his eyes and for a moment he is aware that I am there to provide comfort. He is not afraid and I can sense that he is eager for me to "work my magic," because silently he begins to bargain with me. In his mind he is letting me know that he is tired and ready to "let go" of his earthly body to join those who have gone before him. There are parts of him that are sad about leaving behind those he loves, but after all that he has been through, he finds that he has not an ounce of energy left to give.

My eyes make contact with his and let him know that I understand. I have felt his life speed by in flashes—the memories of love, accomplishments, trials and tribulations. I smiled at the imagery of a little boy dashing down a country dirt road and then felt pride at the man he later became. Glancing down at his wife, I see that she has taken his hand into hers and holds it tenderly. She has fallen asleep next to him, refusing to leave the room even though others have tried relentlessly to encourage her to go home and get some rest. Jumping into her thoughts, I see her fear, her utter devastation about slowly losing the man before her—the love of her life. Gently,

I caress her soul and let her know that I will be with her always and when the time approaches and the moment has come, that I will not waver in my plan to make sure she is supported.

My love for both of them is interrupted by the sound of the nurse as she comes into the room. She approaches the wife asleep in the chair and drapes a blanket around her shoulders, then quietly leaves the room and the couple behind. I notice the sound of the two heartbeats—hers finally relaxed while asleep and his growing fainter and fainter by the moment. Again, I look at the man and slowly approach his bedside. His blue eyes show understanding and he nods as in resignation, giving me permission for what I have to do. And with one last, long drawn out breath, I hold his soul within my own and place it next to my heart. The time has come for us to leave together and I feel gratitude that his broken body lying before me is hurting no more. Just as silently as I arrived, I slip away into the night—my purpose fulfilled. And, no sooner than I have allowed myself to smile at this peaceful ending, I feel the urgent and insistent tug towards another soul. I sit silently in the corner of a new room and wait. The time is coming, but it hasn't arrived just yet.

Death Shouldn't Be a Parade

Perhaps one of the most profound moments I have had as a grief counselor was a particular visit I had with a delightful patient who wished to talk to me about her approaching death. She began by expressing frustration that there were so many friends and family members she had lost contact with or who had abandoned her over the years. Her biggest fear was that as she began the "actively dying" phase of her life, "All of those people will come out of the woodwork and show up to gawk at me lying in my coffin. If they don't care enough to come by and visit me while I am alive, why should they make it a point to come and see me after I am dead?"

She talked about how she loved flowers, peonies to be exact, and wondered why no one seemed to care enough to send her any when she was diagnosed or when she was struggling with devastating treatments that riddled her already weakened body. But she knew that after she died (and she stated this with great sarcasm), that there would be an outpouring of flowers sent to her service and she shook her head at the knowledge that she would not be here, at least physically, to enjoy them. So that is when she made the decision to be cremated and wrote down all of her wishes in the hope that her family would honor them and know that they were doing what she wanted after her death. "Don't place me in a casket and parade people by me," she said. "I want people to remember me as I was, before the sickness and wasting and I want them to remember that my hair was once beautiful and golden." Just being able to have that conversation was relieving and therapeutic. It was one that stuck with me, especially after I began to hear some of the same things from other patients throughout the years.

Sometimes when a loved one is dying, you see an outpouring of support and even a line of people out the door waiting to be admitted to say their "last goodbyes." For others, an approaching death is more quiet, more intimate, with immediate family members only. And still, there are others that unfortunately die alone—with no one present to witness their last breath as they leave their body behind. What I think is important to discuss here is the fact that every family dynamic is different and so, too, is the dying process. For example, one woman spoke to me about how "inappropriate" it was for people to "invade" her home when her husband was dying. She felt like his death should have been private and reserved for just immediate family and didn't understand why everyone felt the need to go walking into their bedroom to lay eyes upon him. As tears rolled down her face, she said, "I felt like he was a float in a parade and he deserved so much better than that."

And yet, there are some families who grow angry and frustrated at friends and loved ones who "don't show up" at the death vigil. Feelings are hurt which often leads to some complicated grief on down the road due to unspoken anger and deep-seated pain caused by miscommunication or misunderstanding. Be cognizant of the intimacy of death. Not everyone wishes to invite you into their inner circle during this most difficult time, so make efforts to be sensitive to their situation. Try not to make assumptions of how others might feel and remember that death is part of our traveling through life—it is not a spectacle, nor should it be made into one. I try to remember conversations shared with me over the years, and I share them with you so that it might make a difference.

Because of these conversations, I was able to set a beautiful white peony on the bed stand of one incredible lady and watch as her eyes danced with gratitude and joy. It bloomed for three straight days and was present for her when she left this world—the flowers that symbolized her love for life were no doubt now clutched in her hands as she made her way to her own parade—the one above the billowing clouds.

Sorting Through a Lifetime of Memories

Everywhere you turn you are inundated with commercials, TV jingles or radio ads encouraging you to "Discover the new you." Diet fads, gyms, and grocery stores encourage you to stop by and try the "next best thing" in hope of obtaining a portion of your money while propelling you toward a life full of changes focused on good health. Many of us are easily duped and find ourselves sucked in by the propaganda and ashamed to admit we have just purchased the latest juicer or book on healthy eating. We are determined that all of our efforts will be rewarded because this year everything is going to be different. And then grief happens.

While the new year may promise so much for so many, there are those who can only look at the flipping of the calendar as an "in your face" reminder that your new year is starting without your loved one. Resolutions that focus on spending more time with family or "getting a fresh start" screams that our loss is present and well-accounted for. Simply finding the motivation to begin somewhere, anywhere, becomes the daily challenge we love to hate. The question many of us face is, "How do I move forward?" Let us look at several examples in the hope that one person's resolution will influence someone else—maybe sending them into a less uncertain future.

Perhaps deciding to go through clothes and belongings, sorting and organizing, is just the ticket for you. Maybe you have been putting off this very emotional task because it creates feelings that you want to ignore. One man expressed that it was hard for him to "give away" his wife's clothes because it made him feel like he was "throwing away pieces of her" and that was too much to bear. A woman found that donating items out-of-town was easier "because I was always worried I would be at the mall or shopping for groceries and run into someone who was wearing my husband's favorite shirt."

The task of emptying boxes, going through drawers or closets, is bound to elicit emotions that will have you crying uncontrollably one moment and then laughing hysterically another. Some people choose to go about this with friends and family, while others savor having the time alone to experience each moment as it comes. What is important to remember is that there should never be a timeline set for when you decide to engage in this activity, nor is there a rule stating that you even have to. However, within many families, there is often a "push" to go through things and divide items that hold special meaning to those involved. This can often be extremely hurtful and should only be done if and when *everyone* is ready. Of course, we can argue that many times we feel as if we will never be ready, but there will come a day when you will know in your heart that the time is right. Also, when we are grieving, we may make a snap decision to hold onto some things and rid ourselves of others. Try to think as carefully as possible about sentimental items before letting them go because once they are gone, it can be difficult to ask for them back.

This past holiday season, my mother spent hours searching her house for my grandmother's cookie cutters. She looked high and low and even had my father join in the task. Finally, she decided that the cutters had to have been lost in their move to Auburn, and quietly resigned herself to letting them go. As a gift, I presented her with a giant box of new cookie cutters, and while she graciously received them, I knew they could never replace the ones that were once held lovingly by my grandmother. Later on, in my own sorting and organizing, lo and behold, I found a *Tupperware* container that held all of those classic cookie cutters. There was the silver star and tin Santa, the red plastic candy cane and snowman—and the memories of making cookies in years past came rushing back. As I called my mother to let her know of my discovery, I thought about all of the time she had spent searching for those and how meaningful they were to her—and are even to this day. I know that the only reason I had them in my possession is because she had given them to me years back, however she had no recollection of having done that and truthfully, neither did I. My point is, when we are on our journey, what may matter to us from one moment to the next can change faster than you can add sprinkles to your sugar cookie. Being able to return that treasure to my mother was priceless.

Taking a Look at Secondary Losses

When death occurs, it can feel like the world stops and everything and everyone moves along without us. We feel stagnant, stuck in a murky place, often struggling to find our way out of that suffocating and painful loss. What most people don't realize is that in addition to the actual death of the person, there are secondary losses that are suffered and can actually be just as painful as the death itself. What are secondary losses and how do they affect the grief journey?

Let's take a look at finances. One of the biggest hardships bereaved people talk to me about is the loss of their spouse's income. Sometimes, the loss is so great that it is impossible to stay in the home that they built their lives in together. When bills and debt become overwhelming, it can impact the grief journey in a negative way, leaving those who are trying their hardest to survive, reeling and full of lost hope. Leaving behind a home, a garden that had been lovingly planted and nurtured over the years, can be devastating. Also, if children are involved, leaving a home due to finances means the possibility of losing their neighborhood friends, their room, their school, their safe places, and maybe even their church community. For those who are in the midst of their grief journey, losses such as these can complicate grief and can quickly dash hopes of survival.

Another secondary loss is the change in social status. With the loss of a spouse, the "couple" status changes and the bereaved is often left out of social events and other occasions in order to avoid awkwardness. To be fair, the bereaved will sometimes avoid spending time with their "couple" friends because being with them has become too painful—a constant reminder of what they once had and what has now been lost. Additionally, if children are involved, suddenly becoming a single parent, handling all the responsibilities of the home and parenting, is new territory. Trying to find your way with the new social status of being single or a single parent is challenging.

Time and time again, it has been stated that the worst part of the grief journey is the devastating loneliness that is experienced. When phone calls stop and the mailbox is empty, or when friends quit extending invitations in order to avoid the discomfort of death, true loneliness sets in and takes root. At times, the bereaved will wonder what they have done for others to forget about them and they often feel lost, hurt, and confused. They express anger at friends that haven't "stopped by," or who haven't called to express condolences and acknowledge that the death occurred. And then, just as quickly, they feel guilty for having those feelings and then angry at themselves for having those thoughts. What can we do for those who are grieving and how can we be supportive?

The most important thing is our presence. If we acknowledge that there are secondary losses and encourage them to talk about how those losses are impacting their grief journey, it will go a long way in the healing process. As the prolific American author, poet, and civil rights activist Maya Angelou stated, "Try to be a rainbow in someone's cloud." At the time, they may not be able to see the gift that you gave them, but one day, it will be remembered as being an absolute treasure.

The Last Dance

While watching an episode of the NBC show *Nashville,* I was overcome by a scene in which family members were on opposite sides of a very difficult issue. A loved one had experienced a massive hemorrhage, was essentially brain dead and on life support. One family member understood that her loved one was "no longer inside that body and her quality of life is gone," and elected to remove all life sustaining measures. The other family member, ripped apart by guilt, was determined to hold on and hope that a miracle was coming, even though no medical results showed viable brain activity or the ability to swallow or breathe on her own. Family member lashed out at family member and the physicians could only stand there and watch helplessly while awaiting a final decision to be made.

As machines were unplugged and tearful goodbyes issued, I watched as a team of doctors hurried to harvest organs in order to provide life for others in need. The family member who made the decision to end life support stood alone and asked for forgiveness, hoping that she had made the best choice for her loved one. The other family member grieved alone at home, consumed with guilt and remorse, angry and quick to blame. I could only wonder what he was going through—how he felt, and if he regretted not being there for his family. And then, I was overcome with memories of situations such as these that I have experienced numerous times over the years while working with hospice. I have watched families come together during these tragic times and I have watched as families have been literally ripped apart. Siblings refuse to talk to each other, children argue over who has "the final say" and there is often resentment if everyone is not on the same page.

Mostly, I see these occurrences happening as a result of our love for the person who is dying. We are so desperate to keep them alive that it often becomes a matter of examining our own issues with death. It is not comfortable nor is it ever meant to be comfortable. However, in times such as these, we must take a step back and ask ourselves, "When does it become about *them* and not about *me?*" If we can ask ourselves this question, we might be able to see that no matter our valiant efforts, the outcome is more than likely going to be the same. And, having our family alongside us instead of against us will create avenues of healing that are more likely to benefit us in the long run.

One of my most vivid memories was of a young man who was actively dying. His family was not convinced that his condition was terminal and they were angry at the world, at God, at physicians, etc. I stepped into his room to help diffuse the situation and this blessed man glanced my way, broke into the widest grin and then proceeded to ask me to dance. He climbed out of bed in his hospital gown, grabbed me into his arms and twirled me about the room, laughing and enjoying every moment. His family, so blinded by their denial, asked, "Does this look like a man that is dying?" He died the next day. It broke my heart that he died knowing how unhappy and angry his family was, however, I drew solace from the fact that I was able to give him a moment of happiness in his final hours. In asking me to dance, he was undoubtedly aware it would be his last, that his dance card was full and that he would leave this world knowing that he would soon be "Dancing with the Stars."

When Helping is Hurting

I had the ultimate privilege to be a part of my beautiful grandmother's last earthly days. She had been married to my grandfather for sixty-seven years and they had both celebrated their ninetieth birthdays. When the decision was made to bring hospice on board, the family, spread out across the U.S., some from as far away as Guam, made the trek to Michigan to gather around the bedside, tell stories, and pass along photo albums. Being the resident counselor and hospice worker, I found myself in many situations that were both difficult and comforting. I was able to use my experience to help my family understand the end of life journey, what to look for, and what to expect along each stage. Many conversations were held about funeral planning and arrangements, careful not to step on anyone's toes or leave anyone out of the decision making. What I was not prepared for was the power struggle amongst the adult children (there are seven plus their spouses) and the expression of anger displayed by my grandfather.

As we know, anger is a healthy emotion and is often expressed during stressful situations, and believe me, this was very stressful for my grandfather. He confided in me that it was very hurtful to him that people were laughing and being loud when "this wonderful and amazing lady was dying in front of him." He was also angry because he felt "forced" into accepting a Home Health worker to give him some relief, allowing him some rest as well as time that he could just *be* with grandma and not feel so overwhelmed. Being the oldest grandchild, I found myself just sitting with him, holding his hand and letting him know that I understood his anger. He felt that caring for grandma was "beautiful" and a "privilege," one he felt he was perfectly capable of handling and he did not appreciate his children making him feel like he wasn't able to care for his wife.

My grandfather is a World War II veteran who spent time at Iwo Jima and is a very proud but humble man. For him, the Lord and his family come first and it was apparent during this exchange that even though he loved his children, he was determined to devote every minute of his time to his wife—never leaving her side and sleeping only when the exhaustion overwhelmed him. Anger and frustration poured from family members who were concerned that their dad was exhausting himself and that he needed to take better care of his health. This is a common reaction from adult children as they cannot fathom the thought of losing both of their parents and so the need to "protect" takes over. But when does this "helping" actually turn into "hurting?"

It is important to remember that the end of life journey is full of emotions and difficult decisions. One thing that is often overlooked, as was the case with my grandfather, is that he was still fully capable of making decisions. When we are forceful in "trying to help," it can create all kinds of chaos and feelings of resentment or frustration. For my grandfather, taking care of his wife was his honor, his privilege—not some health care worker's. Feeling like he had no choice, that he had to give that up, brought him to tears and made him feel like he wasn't capable. It tore at my heart to see him sit alone and broken, the task of caring for his wife given over to someone else. Our family, who had acknowledged that death was approaching and were taking measures to prepare for the moment, lost sight of the fact that my grandfather was still living. Before I left, after kissing my grandmother goodbye, I whispered into my grandfather's ear that he was an amazing caregiver; his love and devotion was evident; his feelings were real, and now that everyone was headed back out of town, he could call and cancel the Home Health worker. I have no doubt that he did just that, and I am certain he was still sitting at her bedside until the very end.

Stepping Stones of Sadness

She sat on the shore and listened to the gurgling of the mighty river as it passed her by—its strength visible and tremendously beautiful. Occasionally, a fish would jump from its depths and cause a loud splash and light ripples would dance across the surface signaling its presence. She sighed at the peace she found when she came here—the place in which they had shared so many memories together over the years. In fact, the ground where she now sat once held their tattered blanket as they enjoyed their first date, a picnic filled with all her favorites. At that memory, tears began to fall.

How difficult it was for her to come here, to be so close to him and yet feel so far away. If she closed her eyes, for the briefest of moments, she could still hear him as he proudly pulled a speckled bass from the water and boasted about it being "the biggest one ever." That was what it was like for her, little moments of absolute joy that would then turn into total devastation leaving her feeling empty and afraid. She came to this spot often not only so she could remember, but also so she could begin living again. In front of her, spread across the width of the river, were the most beautiful rocks she had ever seen. They glistened in the sun and she loved how the light would bounce off of them creating a myriad of colors depending on the time of day. At times she would find turtles or snakes laid out along the tops of the rocks soaking up the rays and absorbing the warmth, an action she envied and longed to once again enjoy.

Since his death, she had battled a constant sense of feeling cold—like she would never be able to be warm again. The absence of her husband, the lack of his presence beside her caused a chill that seemed to reside just beneath her skin and cut her to her very core. Today, she was determined to feel warm again. Glancing to her right she took note of the strength of the water as it rushed by, and then quietly reached down and took off her shoes. Making her way to the edge, she hesitated for just a moment before taking a leap of faith and landing on the first of the many rocks. Its smooth surface felt foreign beneath her feet but welcomed her at the same time and she began to find her confidence.

Stepping ever so lightly, she made her way to the next rock and then the next. When she realized she now stood in the exact center of the river, she squatted down and hugged her knees to her body. To be in this moment with nature, to feel the strength of the water as it brushed against her toes gave her the fortitude to continue. And yet, she was afraid. Afraid of crossing the river of life and finding herself in the welcoming arms of the distant shore. It's not like she hadn't done this hundreds of times, however on this day, the river crossing symbolized so much more to her. It spoke of her strength, her courage, and her need to survive, and it begged her to move forward and find some new meaning in this journey.

Taking the next step, she became less hesitant and actually found herself hopping from rock to rock with more confidence—no longer afraid to fall. With one last step, she felt the cool, green grass as it caressed her skin signaling her arrival. Collapsing, she kissed the ground and sobbed—anguish taking over her senses and allowing her to grieve the loss of her husband. Something about the crossing, the timid stepping across the rocks left her feeling both drained and filled with emotion. For months she could only come to the shoreline, to this place and stare at the water. Today, she was able to conquer the raging waters and use the stepping stones as guides launching her to the other side. And in accomplishing this task, she realized that her grief journey was going to contain numerous stepping stones—some large and flat, others small and sharp. However, if she navigated them correctly, she would learn more about her life and what the future held than if she simply looked forlornly across the river towardthe distant shore. One rock, one step at a time—the journey was hers.

The Beauty of "Soul Passing"

We've all, at one point or another in our lives, experienced it—the passing of a loved one quickly followed by or proceeded by the birth of a new family member. Time and again, I hear people proclaim that "God took one angel while bringing us another." I don't know how to explain why it is that this happens so often, or why it is that people find comfort in this happening, but they do. The pain of the departure from this life of aloved one is difficult to comprehend, but somehow holding onto new life gives us the permission to smile again, to witness the emergence of a new life beginning.

With permission, I have an amazing story to tell—one that will make you stop and think about the beauty of life. A woman in her late eighties, who had led an incredible and very nurturing existence, suffered back-to- back strokes and was essentially nonresponsive. Her daughter chose to have her mom spend her last few days at Bethany House, where she could sit bedside, hold her hand, and have conversations with the mother that raised her and loved her all these years. Her mother was her best friend, and having to watch the strength slowly slip away from her was devastating. However, for fifteen arduous days, she sat and watched and waited. One day slipped into another and the waiting became more and more difficult to bear. Questions were asked. "What is keeping her here? I've given her permission to let go and told her I would be okay." The only response I could give was that we simply didn't know the reason for her continued battle, but that we would soon enough.

We spent a lot of time together over those fifteen days and I learned so much more about what an outstanding lady this was watching over her mother. I found out that she had a grandbaby due in another month or so and how excited she was to see her very first grandchild. I learned about sacrifice, humility, courage and most of all, I watched firsthand the need for support and its importance. Sometimes, when people are in their deepest need, there are "Earthly Angels" that step into our lives and manage to make a difference in our day. I witnessed several of these "Earth Angels" as they came by to hold a hand, bring a meal, or just stopped by to say a prayer or give a kind word. But, nothing prepared me for that final day, day fifteen, the day when I arrived and was met with a smile on the daughter's glowing face.

When I opened up the door to the room, she grabbed my hand and exclaimed, "I know what my mother is waiting for and this time I know in my heart I am right." And then I listened as she proceeded to tell me that her daughter went into labor three weeks early this morning and was currently at the hospital—her first grandchild was about to be born. She said, "Somehow I know momma is watching over that sweet baby and has waited to help guide her safely into this world." And, sure enough, that precious new life entered into the world and within minutes, the fifteen-day battle to hold on was over and her mother took her last breath. We talked about how the two, her mother and her new grandbaby were able to kiss each other as one was entering, the other leaving—a "Soul Passing" if you will. Sometimes it is not up to us to ask "why," nor is there always an answer given when asked; however, in this case, it was clear to see. One loving and nurturing lady was holding on for fifteen days so that she could safely guide the newest family member into this world and kiss her ever so gently on her way out.

Coping with the Calendar

"To have been loved so deeply, even though the person who loved us is gone, will give us some protection forever."

– J.K. Rowling

Searching for Answers in the New Year

After saying goodbye to the sweetest man with whom I had visited a few days before Christmas, I walked to my car clutching an old *Arby's* bag that held a plethora of treasures. During our conversations, he had described the love and craftsmanship he had put into one of his favorite pastimes, the carving of Christmas toys and ornaments as gifts for people who had crossed his path over the years. He talked about the great joy he felt when he was able to gift someone with one of his creations. Since his wife died, he had struggled to find the energy and motivation to spend time in his workshop, and so the wood remained in pieces, silent and uncarved.

This may be a tale that sounds familiar—the loss of interest in activities that we used to enjoy. Things that we loved and engaged in now seem lost and broken, the joy that they brought lies dormant and cold within us. Death brings sadness and it seems to steal our sense of who we are and what we wish to become in a life that now seems empty and worthless without our loved ones present. I mention this because many people feel overwhelmed by the feeling of "loss" but seem more despondent about being "lost." If you think about it, in addition to the death we are facing, there is an overwhelming sense of confusion, of no longer knowing or understanding who we are as individuals. People tell me all the time about feeling no sense of purpose now that their loved one is gone and question why they are still here.

Upon opening a Christmas card from my grandfather, this was this very evident. Though the holiday was quickly approaching, he seemed to be spending more time bargaining "with the man upstairs" about why he was still alive. He seemed frustrated that God didn't seem to be listening to him and expressed his sadness and heartbreak about missing his wife. I share this story, even though it is deeply personal, because his story is not the first of its kind that I hear the last few weeks before Christmas. The holidays are more difficult, especially when newly bereaved, but the same can be said for anytime of the year after a loss. We question who we are and why we are still here; we ponder the meaning of life and try to figure out our purpose for remaining here when we so desperately wish to be with our departed loved ones. My point is that it is quite common to have these thoughts, yet most everyone thinks they are alone in thinking them. They feel guilty for wanting to die and worry that friends and family cannot possibly understand what they are going through.

When I got back to work with my *Arby's* bag, I carefully dumped out all of the handmade creations onto my desk. Wooden tops rolled around in circles, their colors bright and vibrant, each one unique and purposeful. I thought about how those tops spun around and around and I remembered being transfixed as a child, trying to see how long I could make one twirl before it finally came to a stop. With grief, we are sometimes that top—spinning around, going in endless circles and directions that change with each twist of the spindle. Eventually the top will come to a stop and will find itself resting on its side.

Sometimes grief spins us in directions that make us feel dizzy or out of control. We may spin in one direction but then start over and spin in an entirely new one. But, when all the spinning stops, we find ourselves resting and taking measure of the course we have just taken and wondering where we will head next. There is never a guarantee that our journey will be over because there is always a chance someone will give that spindle another twist and send us careening off in yet another direction. However, we do know that eventually the spinning will cease and we can look forward to finding joy in the simplest of pleasures once again. During our lifetimes, we have always been spinning—whether it was in love, in decision making, in laughter or tears—it's just that now we have to learn to spin on our own, temporarily—just until we learn that *we* control the new direction we will soon be spinning.

Holiday Blues: Coping with Our Loss

If I had to identify the one word I hear most often from those who are grieving during the holidays, it would be "escape." With the holiday season in full swing, the need or desire to "escape" from all of the memories and traditions lurking around every corner becomes an elusive task that hardly anyone seems able to conquer. And, after just experiencing "Fall Back" and realizing that our days are now going to be shorter and our evenings longer, it is inevitable that we begin to recognize the darkness of grief that surrounds and entombs us in its nightly grasp. For many, the holidays are filled with wonder, excitement and family gatherings. But for others, it creates an atmosphere of loss and longing, sometimes sending us into a downward spiral of grief that is difficult to comprehend.

For friends and family members, I want to stress the importance of communication around the holiday season. Feelings are raw and there is confusion as to what to do or how to do it. One gentleman shared how difficult it was for him to face Thanksgiving because it was a huge family gathering, one that he and his wife had always enjoyed. Without her here, he is unsure whether or not he wants to continue the tradition—simply put, he is "not sure if he is ready." But, on the flipside, his children are desperate to keep traditions the same. They feel strongly about getting together, and see it as a way to honor their mother. This is part of what makes the holidays so hard. Even though everyone is grieving, the way in which we grieve and how we choose to share it with others differs across the board, even within family systems.

The positive thing is that if we so choose, we can take some time to talk about our wants and needs and create a plan of action to best face the holiday season. We may sometimes differ on what is important to us and how we choose to celebrate and that is okay. We don't always have to agree, but we must choose what is going to be the most comfortable situation for us. We may be tempted to do what others want us to do, thus sacrificing our own needs for the benefit of others. That is also okay, but remember that ultimately, the choice is yours and yours alone.

Coping With the Holidays

It is happening already; stores are filling the aisles with holiday treats and decorations, and Christmas music is playing softly in the background. Even if we were not grieving, just the sights and sounds of what is about to come could be overwhelming and stressful. And, if we are currently on a grief journey, leaving the comfort of our homes only to be confronted on every street corner with holiday cheer and ho-ho-hos can send us running back to our homes wanting not to go out again until it is all over. I just sat and listened to someone newly bereaved who stated that she just wanted to cancel the holidays; everyone expected her to cook and be joyful and she just didn't want to celebrate this year. I assured her that she was having a very normal response to a very painful event and I gently encouraged her to take some time and think about things before making any final decisions; there was still time to change her mind.

Many people ask questions about how to prepare for the holiday season. They want to know if they should cancel traditional plans since it would be too painful to endure; they want to know if it would be appropriate to leave town to avoid friends and family; and they want to know if there is anything they can do to make the holidays easier. What I truthfully tell them is that the holidays are going to be hard; the loss of our loved ones is even more evident, making us painfully aware that they are not physically present with us; and most importantly, there is simply no way to avoid it altogether. I advise them to communicate with family and friends, to let them know what would or would not be helpful, and then to formulate a plan that takes into account the raw, fresh feelings of hurt and loss.

One of the ways we can prepare for the holidays is to look throughout the community for programs and services created to help us during this difficult time. Some area churches hold services for the bereaved, a powerful and healing way to still celebrate but in an environment with others also traveling the grief path. Many funeral homes offer services as well and they are very good at reaching out to the families they have served and letting them know that they care about them and their loved one. My hospice company partners with a local funeral home to sponsor an annual event called "Coping With the Holidays, A Day of Remembrance." The program begins with a free luncheon and features speakers, who are also on the grief journey, offering words of healing and hope in preparation for the next few months. That evening, we gather for "Light the Night," a candle lighting ritual that takes place behind a local hospice house. During this time, we come together as a community to honor our loved ones, light candles, and walk in their memory. It is a time of sharing and healing, and it serves to provide comfort by being with others during their time of loss and sorrow.

Cupid's Sorrow

Valentine's Day brings the overwhelming onrush of radio spots and TV ads encouraging you to purchase decadent chocolates and bouquets of roses. Love is in the air and Cupid is rapidly letting his arrows fly toward unsuspecting targets, hoping to create a new "Love Connection." Michelangelo, one of the greatest artists of all time, once created a piece of art depicting Cupid lying down asleep, a representation of absent love or sorrow. For those who are traveling the path of grief, the image of love and its absence looms large. When everyone around you is talking about candy hearts and Hallmark cards, the only heart that really matters is yours, and it is shattered and broken, the grief journey brutal and harsh.

Because the holiday itself is unavoidable, I would encourage you to take some time to be present with the lost love of your life on that day. Presence is a wonderful gift that we give not only to others, but to ourselves as well. Being mindful and creating an atmosphere of acceptance of our grief is of the utmost importance. Yes, our loved ones are not physically present to share our affections, but they do continue to live within us if we are open to a continued life with them being spiritually present. Romance is something that breathes inside of us. We learn from early on to address cards to classmates and deliver them into brightly decorated shoeboxes. The opening of each card is wondrous and full of excitement, the day filled with abundances of sugar, cupcakes, and secret admirers. As we grow older, the holiday takes on a deeper meaning—one of courtship and closeness. Soon, we find ourselves engaged and then married to the person of our dreams, determined to live out our lives with the person who made our hearts whole. And them death occurs, the heart ruptures into a thousand pieces, and romance seems lost forever.

For this Valentine's Day, I would like you to think about your lifetime of love and romance with your beloved one. Pull out old cards that you may have saved, love letters, or even a special gift that holds significant meaning. Take the time to be present with each of those items, those memories, and relive them. Yes, this will be painful, but it will also be a means to honor them and a tribute to the love that you shared together. Indulge in your favorite box of chocolates, envision Cupid's arrow once again finding its way to your heart. Hold onto a special thought and be present today in the memory of your love. It is a holiday for lovers and for romance, so put on some soft music and recall your first dance. Sometimes, if we just close our eyes, we can envision them being beside us. Too many times, we let others make us feel like we can no longer talk about our grief, our sadness, or our feelings of loss. Let this Valentine's Day be a reminder to our friends and family that even when a death occurs, it doesn't mean that our love and romance dies with that person. Choose to embrace this holiday with an open heart, an open mind, and open eyes. Love is in the air and all around you on this day—celebrate their love for you and remember that your love for them lives on forever. XOXO

Love, Loss and Mother's Day

From the time that I can remember, Mother's Day was always filled with excitement. My brothers and I would plan a special breakfast in bed, slathering toast with butter or simply pouring cereal into a bowl. Sometimes we would find a wildflower in the yard and place it alongside the plate, a garnish to brighten our mother's day. As kids, we did not have any money so we decorated handmade cards and wrote poems that described how we had the best mother in the world. We tried our best to surprise her, and yet as an adult, I now know that she would sit patiently in her bed waiting for us, listening as we whispered in the kitchen, fully aware of our escapades, ready to eat the now cold toast and the soggy cereal with the biggest smile on her face. In essence, that is what most mother's do—they sacrifice and pour out unconditional love; they hold no judgment and are quick to give praise and feedback that lifts the spirits.

It is difficult for many people as Mother's Day approaches. I have spoken to numerous people who have expressed anxiety and profound sadness knowing what they will experience for the first time without their mother on Mother's Day. Some are hopeful that the day will pass by quickly, while others are planning on celebrating their mother's lives, either with a big family meal or gathering, or quiet time spent thinking over all the wonderful memories they have shared across the years.

What is often overlooked during this time is what our children face after the death of their mother. I have met with several kids who were all having a "difficult" week according to their family. In speaking with the kids individually, I discovered that at each one of their schools, classes were busy making Mother's Day gifts. And, for each child, there was immediate sadness and then confusion as to what to do "because their mother had died." I let them each know that even though his/her mother was physically gone, that she would always live in their heart. I encouraged them to make their mother a gift anyway—one that they could then present to another member of the family, take to the cemetery, or keep for themselves. We talked about the love that they have for their mother and then I reminded them that it is okay to be sad.

Sometimes, our feelings are overlooked in the excitement of a celebration. It is hard to be mindful of others and the grief path that they are traveling if we have not been touched by loss. Remember that there are many friends and family members who are struggling with the loss of their mother on Mother's Day—even though it may have been months or even years since the death, the fact of the matter is that it still hurts. One thing I have always known for sure and treasured is the unconditional love a mother has for her children. Mothers help guide us when we are lost, hug us when we are hurting, and give us stern lessons when we need direction. Mothers love us from the moment of conception, nurturing us within their bodies, awaiting our arrival. Some research states that we know the voice of our mothers even in utero, and we begin to develop an unbreakable bond even then, one that continues throughout our lifetime.

When we experience the death of our mother, it is hard to express the sadness that we are feeling as the sense of loss is overwhelming. We remember all of the times shared, the memories lived and our hearts burst with the loss of the first person on earth who knew we existed. I encourage you to take some time on Mother's Day to cherish your mother, whether alive or deceased. Spend some time thinking about all the sacrifices, the hugs and kisses, the long conversations and timely advice given when needed. I am a firm believer that even in death, our mothers live within us and continue to guide us when we least expect it, but definitely when we need it the most. I was actually born on Mother's Day and have always joked that it was the best gift I could have ever given my mother. Gifts are often given out of love and thoughtfulness, and because of my mother and the gifts she has given me, I will be sure to celebrate with her—not only on this earthly plane, but when it is her time, on the heavenly plane as well. Happy Mother's Day, moms.

Tears, Traditions and a Side of Turkey

One of my favorite songs from the musical *Les Miserables* is entitled "Empty Chairs at Empty Tables." It is a ballad that memorializes all of those who sacrificed their lives in battle, taking note of the places at the table that now stand empty, their presence no longer there. At every Thanksgiving, I am reminded of this song because it is always apparent that we are missing loved ones who are deceased, their empty places at our tables are glaring and difficult to comprehend. I have mentioned that it is common for us to try and "escape" moments such as these around the holidays, but the honest truth is that no matter how hard we try, it remains almost impossible. The holidays will arrive and they will depart and soon we will be beyond the point of yet another difficult moment that at the time we did not think we could survive.

Recently, a gentleman shared within a group setting that he was most anxious about the upcoming holiday because he was afraid he might experience "joy." Just the thought of this possibility, that he might enjoy the pleasure of family and fellowship, brought about tremendous feelings of guilt—that perhaps he was being dishonorable to the woman he loved. As heads bobbed around the room, it was apparent that many were feeling the same way. Feelings of guilt around the holidays sometimes outweigh the sadness and despair that we harbor. As the bereaved, it is sometimes difficult to fathom that we can ever be happy again, and finding ourselves in situations where there is laughter or enjoyment can often propel us into berating ourselves for simply "having a good time." By the same token, there are those who will be quick to tell us that we shouldn't feel guilty, that we should embrace "joy," however, sometimes we are so despondent and broken from our loss that no matter how hard we try, it just does not seem possible.

I read a quote recently that spoke to me. "When your heart is broken, make art out of all the pieces." When we fall down and the pieces are all around us, we must make sure we pick something up as we stand back on our feet. Grief is like this every single day—we feel lost and broken, we stumble and fall, but each time we learn something about ourselves—what we can handle and what we cannot. Each time we pick up one of those pieces, it proves to us that we are surviving, even if it may feel like we are barely breathing.

This holiday season, I wish to encourage you to consider your family traditions, customs and desires. Communicate your needs amongst your friends and family and only embrace what is most comfortable for you. Tears are going to be a factor, that is inevitable, as we are sure to find ourselves weeping over memories, our hearts ripe with the last moments we shared with our loved ones. No matter where we look, the fact remains that there will be empty chairs at our tables this year. Perhaps we can fill that chair with thoughts of things that we are thankful for, or memories of times spent in holidays past. Keep in mind that no matter what, it is going to hurt, but this is the kind of hurt that will ensure our growth. Turkey and all the fixings are just a small part of what this holiday means to us—it also means family and honoring the memory of those we loved and lost. When it comes down to the family gathering or selecting our favorite recipes on our plates, hold dear the imprint our loved ones have made on our lives and let it enrich our souls. Oh, and if you would please, pass that pumpkin pie.

A Sad Silent Night

Silent night, holy night! All is calm, all is bright ... except for on this night, and the many nights leading up to the holiday season for those who are grieving. While most of us are running around purchasing last minute gifts and trying to prepare for the countless family and friends who may be visiting this year, for many it will be quiet and lonely. As a grief counselor, it is hard to witness the absolute devastation that grief renders upon those who have just lost a loved one. And their stories ... well, let's just say that they are both beautiful and crushing at the same time. There is nothing more beautiful than listening about the love and adoration for a love lost, however in that beauty and the telling of it, it can be overwhelming to share in the loss they are experiencing.

At a recent support group, the topic of holidays came up and several members were adamant that they didn't wish to have anything to do with the season at all; they didn't feel like celebrating and could not care less what anyone else thought. Others were determined to celebrate, choosing to pull out all of the decorations and shiny tinsel, in memory of their loved ones. What is important to remember is that there is no right or wrong way in any of this—to celebrate or not celebrate. When death occurs, this is the one time that everyone can be given a "bah humbug" card for free because guess what? Grief can steal all of our holiday joy even faster than the Grinch riding away from Whoville. That is a fact.

Sometimes, even when we are not aware, the holiday season allows us to continue our grief work. Because everything is so front and center, grief triggers are sure to arise when we least expect them and even appear to lie in wait for us around every corner—like a thief waiting to steal any single moment where we feel as though we might be "doing okay." Time and time again, people share with me that they are overwhelmed by the holidays, that there is no escape from all of the memories of times spent with their loved ones. They talk about the need to fast forward and "put the holiday behind me" and yet, we know that is simply not possible. I like to encourage time spent immersing themselves in those memories, allowing themselves to process and grieve. For some, this is unfathomable and even loathsome because just the thought of experiencing that kind of pain makes them want to run in the opposite direction, and who could blame them? Pain hurts. It makes us feel things that we may not be ready for and let's face it, who enjoys embracing pain?

I am reminded of a sweet person who described themselves as being a Scrooge over the years, never wanting to decorate or put up a tree. This Christmas season, she spent an entire weekend sorting through boxes and lovingly unwrapping each and every ornament that had been given to her over the years. She wept as she relived traveling on a sailboat for the trip she had once taken with her love, and laughed at the pictures of them at the county fair that she had placed within a tiny heart frame. Each item held special meaning to her and even though it felt like her heart was going to burst with each unwrapping, she cherished every single moment of reliving her holidays past with her loved one. And when she was through, she sat down at the kitchen table with a warm mug of hot chocolate and gave thanks for those memories. If we are able, finding time to do this kind of grief work can be very healing. Again, it is not easy, however it does allow us to be in touch with the parts of our soul that are desperate to feel love. Grief creates many "silent nights," but, there is also the knowledge that our loved ones will forever and always be "sleeping in heavenly peace."

The Christmas Cardinal

Earlier in the year, I distinctly remember being overwhelmed by a grief trigger that came out of nowhere. Grief triggers often happen that way—we are feeling good without a care in the world one moment, then gasping for breath and trying to stay upright the next. I was drinking my morning cup of coffee and enjoying the sunrise when I was surprised by the sight of about eight stunning cardinals perched upon the magnolia tree in my backyard. These redbirds have always been a favorite of mine, but never had I witnessed so many in one location at any given time. I recalled that redbirds are mostly independent and don't often fly or group together, so seeing them gathered in one place literally took my breath away.

As a grief counselor, I have always harbored a fondness for the red cardinal as it is seen by many as a messenger from the afterlife, a "hello from above" if you will, from our departed loved ones. It seems that throughout my life, I would catch a glimpse of one of these beautiful birds when I seemed to be in need of receiving a message and always at just the perfect time. Many people have shared stories with me of "messages" like these and I am always comforted when hearing them. I know in my heart that when we are open to receiving messages, we are more likely to smile from the instant healing that takes place from having received them.

Years ago, my grandfather retired in Florida and couldn't sit still—always thinking, planning and doing, bouncing from one hobby to the next. He learned how to make golf clubs and cuckoo clocks, and grew orange trees in his backyard. All of those things brought him great joy, but it was the last hobby that he worked so hard at, that wound up leaving a lasting impression on me. He chose to learn the art of making stained glass. Right before he died, he completed his first piece, a beautiful circle of colors that featured at its center, the red cardinal. I remember being fascinated by the way the light lit up the wings and as it swayed in the wind, it appeared as if the bird was literally taking flight. After he died, I remember the first time I came back to visit my grandmother and how overbearing the sadness was for all of us. The house felt so empty and silent without him there. And yet, it also felt alive—his presence was in every item he created and the trees in the yard were filled with ripened fruit—fruit that he nurtured and harvested every year. But, nothing stood out to me more than that incredible piece of stained glass. It seemed to call to me, my eyes transfixed by its alluring beauty.

Both my grandmother and my grandfather are now gone and I am honored to say that the glass red bird now resides in my home. Every day, I watch as the light changes its appearance and I am reminded of my grandfather's workmanship and his kind spirit. I used to wonder why he chose a red cardinal as his first and only piece. Then, I realized that it was meant to be a reminder to my grandmother after he died, that he would always be there, watching over her. Today, he watches over me and my family and he lets me know that he is present. Whenever I catch a glimpse of red flitting about my yard, or alighting upon a tree as I am driving, I am comforted in the knowledge that I have many family members and friends who are interested in stopping by to say hello. And, as they take flight and catch the wind, I smile to let them know that I felt blessed and enjoyed their visit.

Calling on Compassion

"Although it's difficult today to see beyond the sorrow, may looking back in memory help comfort you tomorrow."

– Unknown

A Blessing of Watermelons

Every once in awhile, I receive what I like to call a "message from above" telling me I need to be at a certain place at a certain time. On one particular occasion, I was driving back into town after having made a bereavement visit and was thinking about the hardships this family was already facing, when all of a sudden, I received one of those messages. I cannot explain this, except maybe as a "tug" that pulls me in a certain direction, and on this day it was towards a nearby thrift store. As the exit was quickly approaching, I looked into the rearview mirror and saw that the way was clear for me to cross over safely and leave the highway. Almost always, when this happens, I find one of the most amazing treasures, somebody else's "junk" that becomes one of my prized possessions.

Entering the store, I browsed up and down the aisles and finally stopped to look at a giant wicker basket that was wedged under the bottom shelf. After some tricky maneuvering, I was able to extract the basket and open up the lid. Inside was a plethora of everything watermelon that you could ever ask for: watermelon plates, cups, baskets, placemats, lemonade pitchers, chip and dip holders, etc. The picnic set was incredible and one I knew would be well-loved by my family. I searched for an employee to help me identify a price and was pleasantly surprised when I was told "$10.00" That basket was quickly snatched up and carried to the front counter with a smile on my face. I was filled with wonder at how once again I had benefitted from that "tiny voice" that led me to this store on this day. However, what happened next is the neatest part of the story.

The sweet lady who helped me happened to notice that I worked for a local hospice. She then began to weave for me a story that took place over fifteen years ago, when her mother was diagnosed with a terminal illness and was to be one one of the first patients admitted to a new hospice house. With silent tears rolling down her face, she described the peace and love her family had after touring the facility and their faith in knowing that it was a place they wanted their mother to be at the end of her life. But, as we all know, death has its own timetable and her mother died a few days before the hospice house opened its doors. She talked about how Octobers are hard for her every year, and so I invited her to call me in October and then come to our candle lighting service behind that same hospice house in November to give her a chance to honor her mother. She came out from behind the counter to hug me and said, "It was meant to be for us to meet today."

Walking out to my car, I was astounded at all the events that had to have happened for this connection to have been made and shook my head in awe. I have mentioned in previous columns that if we are but open to messages from above, we are more likely to receive them. And after placing my basket of watermelon stuff into the car, I heard the message loud and clear. The message became even clearer the next morning, after arriving at work, when a co-worker explained to me that the watermelon picnic basket used to belong to her husband's mother. After his mother's death, he kept it for a time but realized it would be better off with a family that would use it and love it as much as his mom did. I couldn't help but smile at this wonderful circle of life, of events that happened and how everything was made possible by that "inner voice" that tugged me off the road in the direction I was led on that particular day. This weekend, I plan to serve up a well-prepared meal on watermelon plates with the knowledge that they were once loved dearly and are still "in the family."

Finding Answers after an Unexpected Death

So many times, I hear it in their voices and I see it in eyes that stare at me with troubled expressions—the look and sound of loss and confusion. For some of us, death is expected, especially when facing a long illness. But, for others, death comes suddenly and often leaves us stumbling around in vain trying to make sense of what has happened. No where is this more certain and profound than after facing the death of a loved one due to suicide. Over the years, the act of suicide has become more visible in our society, no longer hidden away as an act of shame or considered taboo or off limits for discussion. With the emergence and power of social media, society is recognizing that many are suffering in silence, and it is only in their death that we become painfully aware of all the things that are broken and then wonder how on earth we could have possibly missed them.

After the death of Robin Williams, America's "Funny Man," it became readily apparent that suffering is not always visible, even to those who know us and love us best. His act of suicide brought forth a new level of education and understanding that many had previously avoided. Never stopping to think about what suicide means or how it affects others simply because it had never touched theirr life or planted itself upon their doorstep. The death of a man so revered and loved for his humor and the way he made others laugh, confused many and brought about countless questions of "why?" or "how could this happen to someone so full of life?"

When I am present for a bereaved family after the shocking act of suicide, I am often overwhelmed by the anguish, the confusion, and the guilt they face. Questions run rampant through their minds as they wonder what they could have done differently, or if they even could have prevented this from happening. One thing that stands true is that the act of suicide doesn't take away the pain, as it basically just gives it to someone else—those who are left behind to pick up the pieces. It is a hurt that is indefinable, especially when there are no answers provided, no explanations or heartfelt letters or notes explaining the decision to end a life. And, for many, grief becomes more complicated because it is not just the death that one is grieving—it is the unanswered questions and the constant wondering about what could have been.

Grief is terrible. It is a brutal and honest truth that we must all face at one time or another. But when we have to face a death that has more questions than answers, it can create a tailspin of doubt, self-blame and terrible guilt. Even if, after the act of suicide, everything was all laid out nice and neat and there was an explanation, this only goes a short way toward healing the broken hearts of family. It is important to remember, that like all grief, it is encouraged that yoy share the journey with others versus trying to carry it alone. A loved one's suicide can be emotionally devastating, and so as you prepare to face your life without them, try to incorporate the use of healthy coping strategies—such as seeking support—to begin the journey to healing and acceptance. If you are a close friend, it is important to be supportive and present.

As Robin Williams was quoted, "I used to think the worst thing in life was to end up all alone, it's not. The worst thing in life is to end up with people that make you feel all alone." For the person or individual who commits suicide, the hurt and the pain is final. For those left behind, it is only the beginning of a long journey—one that creates more questions than answers, and one that requires a nurturing and loving acceptance of the hurt both from ourselves and from others.

The Loneliest Journey

I knocked softly on the door and was greeted once again by a gentle and beautiful lady, one whose face showed confusion and anxiety at my appearance at her residence. She quickly attempted to cover that up and smiled, inviting me into her one bedroom apartment at an Assisted Living complex. I introduced myself to her, explaining that every week she asks me to do so, and she laughed the laughter of a small child who has just experienced the joy of cotton candy for the very first time. We sat facing each other in her tiny space and quietly observed the hummingbirds darting to and fro outside her window. After some time, she spoke, "Well, here I am ... just sitting in the chair of "do nothing." When asked if she had attended any of the activities down the hall, she was unable to remember. When asked if she enjoyed spending time with her peers at breakfast, she stated that she probably did but was unable to tell me if that was true or not. And then, she grabbed my hand, held it tight and started to cry.

Her story was not uncommon, but it was one that touched my heart to the very core. It was a story of anguish and pain, grief and loss ... but perhaps most glaring, was her feeling of abandonment. She shared how she felt like her diagnosis altered the way people interacted with her, as if she was unable to hold an adult conversation. She provided descriptions of people who would raise their voice as if she were deaf instead of challenged with memory loss; people who treated her as if she was a child, unable to perform basic tasks; and those who left her alone for long periods of time simply because they didn't think she would remember them being there. All of these things weighed heavy on her heart as she poured out her feelings, thanking me over and over again for "taking the time out of my busy schedule to come and visit an old lady like me." I was quick to assure her that my time with her each week was one of the highlights of my day, it was meaningful and filled with knowledge that only she could teach me. She got a kick out of that and then proceeded to share more about her daily experiences and how they have impacted her life.

One of the things that I adore about her is that she is very blunt and incredibly sassy. She likes to do her own hair and make-up and she pays careful attention to her outfit selection. For her, these are important things—things she still has control over, and once they are done in the morning, she struggles to fill the rest of her day. True, there are countless friends that stop by to love on her and take her places, but they are not her blood family. She grieves for lost family and is still keenly aware of their absence, the memory of their deaths sharp and vivid in her mind. She finds herself overwhelmed with sadness throughout the day and emphatically states that, "There is no lonelier journey than that of slowly losing your mind, your memories, your way of doing things, and eventually your life." I squeeze her hand in mine as I tell her that her present life has meaning and a purpose— that she is still able to smile and share the most amazing stories from her childhood. Her eyes seek out mine to see if I am telling the truth, and she confirms that I am genuine in my efforts to comfort her. My goal for this visit is to bring her some semblance of joy, even if it is but for a moment, and to let her know that she matters. At our parting, she reminds me to re-introduce myself to her again next week and, as always, I promise that I will. She releases me from a hug that screams, "Don't leave me," and I struggle to walk away knowing that she is already starting to feel the loneliness of abandonment yet again.

There are countless numbers of people whose struggle with Alzheimer's Dementia bears a close resemblance to the story you have just read. Halls in nursing homes and Assisted Living facilities are filled with those who grapple with the day-to-day challenges facing them, and are often only visited or spoken to by the employees who work there. Wouldn't it be amazing if we could all stroll down the halls and take the time to be impactful on someone's life? True, they may not remember us, but at least for that moment, they would feel as if they mattered ... and isn't that the most important thing?

The Stranger in the Mirror: A Different Level of Grief

After being released from a huge hug, this sweet lady looked at me intently and whispered, "It was so nice of you to come by and see me. Please introduce yourself to me again when you come back next week because I know I won't remember you." The joy and sadness that reflected in her eyes literally crushed my heart as I watched her struggle with her memory loss and her ability to remember those around her that have loved and cared about her. She is a shell of who she once was and she exists within a small apartment, trapped within a mind that she feels has betrayed her. For those of you who have experienced the devastation of Alzheimer's Disease, or any other form of the disease, you will be able to relate to the fears and frustrations that are sure to develop alongside this dreaded illness.

For her, she talks candidly about the woman she "used to be." She describes a simple farm girl that wound up marrying a wonderful man who pampered and spoiled her. She talks about his death, the unexpected and tragic death of several of her children, and then she talks about how her grief was heightened when she began to lose one of the most important parts of herself ... her memory. The grief is evident, the depression rolls across the lines of her face and she weeps about all that she has lost. A book sits bedside her, untouched, "because I know I love to read, but if I am really enjoying a chapter and then set it down and come back to it later, I haven't a clue what is going on." Her apartment holds a few treasured mementos from her life, pictures line the walls and at this point, she is still able to identify the smiling faces looking back at her from those frames. She understands that this too will fade over time and the thought of that creates an overwhelming sense of anxiety and loss.

What many have come to understand when dealing with this disease is that it robs you. It is terrifying to wake up one day and realize that you don't remember the day before or the person who has just walked into your room. As caregivers, it is difficult to watch our loved ones struggle to hold onto their memories and their sense of self. When they become aware that their memory is fading, they attempt to grapple with the idea that soon they will lose everything that is dear to them and that their loved ones can only sit by and watch it all happen. Feelings of guilt, loss, anger, sadness, and the idea of "being a burden" run through their minds, and caregivers struggle to stay positive and hopeful while coming to terms with an illness that is hard to understand.

One of the most important things to remember is that even though memory is fading, and a loved one or friend appears to be slipping away from you, there is still a person within that skin—a human being that craves presence, a touch on the hand, a card or a kind word. Yes, they may not know who you are or remember the fact that you were there yesterday, but having contact with others can lift their spirits in ways that will erase sadness from the eyes and light up a face for miles. Remembering is the act of recalling information or reliving old stories. Remembering is also an opportunity for us to take some time for reflection, to recognize that there are those who feel trapped inside their own skins, lost or locked away behind closed doors. Finding ways to reach out to them and to the caregivers that lovingly tend to them daily, is a challenge that we must face head on, because in doing so, we will create new memories for ourselves—memories of being loving and gentle towards those who need our kindness. That is the kind of memory that touches lives and will comfort our hearts forever.

A Graveside Tribute

Shortly after submitting the column that referenced her, my sweet grandmother passed away quietly and peacefully in her home; and yes, my grandfather was there by her side. Many of us had just arrived back at homs, and quickly made plans to travel back to Michigan to be with family. The journey along the way was filled with wonderful discussions and stories about "times when we were little" and "do you remember whens." I particularly love the memory of grandma's house full of angels—standing sentry in every corner, filling every nook and secret hideaway—given to her over the years by her children, grandchildren, and great-grandchildren. I loved the crooked finger she would chase us with if one of our pillow fights drew dangerously close to a china cabinet or mantel piece—the angels tipping precariously close to the edge of their demise (I swear she had eyes in the back of her head). Memories are wonderful but they both hurt and bring comfort. Let me comment further on one of the most important memories I have of my grandmother—the love she had for her family.

We are a large and close family (grandma was one of eleven children, my dad was one of seven, and I am one of five). My grandparents always taught us that being together and spending quality time with one another is the most important gift we could ever give them. As children, we never truly understood this, but as adults, that lesson has led us to make these same truths a priority in our own families. Nothing shows the strength and the power of family like losing a loved one. As a family, we rallied; we rallied around grandpa, we took care of the music selections and picked photos that told the story of my grandmother's life. Everyone that wanted to have a role in the honoring of my grandmother was welcome to do so, but nothing was more special to me than each of her twenty-two grandchildren carefully selecting a "special angel" from grandma's collection. Looking in that cabinet was hard, but the ritual of picking one that meant something to me was powerful. Seeing those angels at the funeral home surrounding her with love was overwhelming but healing. Being able to take mine home afterwards was an honor.

I close by sharing something that I have never shared before; a moment that will forever burn in my memory like the fiery spirit that took over me at that time, allowing me to share with others the love of my grandmother. With red rose in hand, and prayers being read at the graveside, I was suddenly filled with the need to sing. And sing I did—the words of "How Great Thou Art" spilled out of me loud and true, the tears silently rolling down my face. Suddenly I realized that everyone else was singing along with me, including my grandfather, and the smile he had on his face at that moment was one I will never forget. I know that my grandmother was smiling down on us from heaven (our new angel), singing along with us, because after all, it was her favorite song—*Then sings my soul, my Savior God, to Thee, How great Thou art! How great Thou art!*

Today, my porcelain angel sits in a special place in my home. She stands sentry over my family and gives me daily reminders of the love my grandmother impressed upon all of us.

A Phone Call Away

She sat in the group and listened as those around her shared some of the most difficult aspects of their grief journey. Several times she attempted to speak, but hesitated due to the outpouring of tears that closed her throat and prevented her from uttering a word. Then, someone else spoke to exactly how she was feeling and everything came pouring out at once—the loss of her father, his upcoming death anniversary, and most importantly the absolute hollow feeling she felt every morning at 6:20 a.m. when he was supposed to call. For her, mornings were the hardest because time seemed to stand still around the exact moment the phone used to ring—his voice hardy and filled with worldly advice on how she should go about her day. With his death, the absence of that familiar ring made starting her day difficult and she longed to hear her father's voice just one last time.

Many people share stories such as these and each one is as heart breaking as the next. In addition to the actual physical loss of our loved one, we lose the everyday contact and conversations we are used to having. It is not unusual for someone to pick up the telephone, dial the number and wait for their loved one to answer before they realize that no one is there to pick up the phone. They feel horrified that they engaged in this action thinking that something is wrong with them, that they are going crazy because "How could I forget that they died? What is wrong with me?" When this comes up during an individual session, I try to validate for them that this is a normal part of grief and that many people find themselves doing the exact same thing. Sometimes they breathe huge sighs of relief, but other times they look at me like I am just feeding them a line. "Normal" people don't do things like call someone who has died.

When this comes up within a group setting, it is much easier for people to find relief because almost everyone has experienced the exact same thing or at least something quite similar—walking down the hall to dispense medications, setting their plate at the table, checking on them before bed, etc. Again, it's not that we are in denial that the death happened—it is glaringly evident. I think that our grief allows us to experience the loss in many different ways, and some are just more hurtful than others. But when it comes to picking up that phone and hitting speed dial—sometimes we find ourselves just waiting to hear their voice come across the answering machine. We cling to the receiver and hit play again and again until our need at that moment is satiated and we are able to put it away until the next time.

Nothing can replace our loved ones—their voice, their laughter, or the advice given when we need it the most. And nothing can take away the hurt that we feel in knowing that their actual voice will not be waiting for us on the other end when we call. Just know that if something like this this has ever happened to you, it is perfectly normal. What is unpleasant is when someone calls asking to speak with the person who has died and you are forced into the unpleasant task of telling them that they are no longer here. One group member shared, "Verizon called the other day asking for my husband, saying he was ready for an upgrade. At first I was stunned, but then I let them know that he got an upgrade all right—he had died and no longer needed phone service." Though everyone chuckled at her good sense of humor about it, it was easy to see the hurt that can come about from these unexpected calls. Let us remember that even though we might not be able to dial their number and hear them say, "Hey there" or whatever the telltale line that was their signature, grief support is just a phone call away. As AT&T used to say, "Reach out and touch someone."

Age is Only a Number

When I received the call from a distraught family member saying that her mother was having a "really difficult time" with the death of her husband, I gathered a couple of thoughts to process for a later time. What I wondered was what defines a "really difficult time?" And, what needs to happen for individuals to realize that asking for help and/or support is a sign of strength, not one of weakness? Almost every time I find myself in the presence of someone who is grieving, there is always an apology given for what they feel is an imposition. Even though I make it clear to them that grief support is my passion and that meeting with those who are on their grief journey is a privilege, I still find that I have to give people permission to ask for help.

With this in mind, I spent my drive to visit this sweet lady in quiet contemplation, wondering what I would find when I arrived and how to even begin processing grief with someone who was so well-versed and seasoned in life. This incredible person was ninety-nine-years-old and had recently celebrated her seventy-fifth wedding anniversary with her husband who, in his own right, had lived to be one hundred and two. What could I possibly say or do to comfort this precious soul who stared at me with the deepest despair, her eyes pleading with me to impart some words of wisdom that would make everything better? Just as always, I knew that my presence in her home was perhaps the greatest gift she could have received—that her loneliness and the need to talk about her husband and their life together would be the beginning of one of the most incredible days I had ever experienced.

She started by asking me if I liked to read and when I responded with a resounding yes, she slowly made her way across the room and brought to me a book she had written at the grand age of ninety-seven and had published. She pointed out the picture of her husband on the front cover all dapper in his fine suit and then laughed at the hairstyle she wore "back in the day." Through her trip down memory lane, she grew more animated at stories she would remember and then would take a long poignant pause to gather herself when some of those memories would steal her breath and make her clutch her chest, signifying the hurt and pain she was feeling at that moment. And as she recalled each story, the life of the woman before me began to take shape and the love of her husband and their life together became the actual story.

I sat on the couch and attempted to soak everything in—to accept the gift that was being given to me—aa I quietly listened. At one point, she stopped talking, grew flustered and asked, "Would you like a glass of tea?" She apologized for not having offered sooner and I was quick to let her know that I was not thirsty, politely declining her offer, and urging her to continue where she had left off. Even though I spent several hours there and knew I would be back to visit her again, the story of her life was breathtaking; but the weight of her grief and the story she had yet to share about her loss was the subject matter she was trying most to avoid. Again she apologized to me, and this time it was because she felt like she had wasted my time by spending so much time "rattling on about myself." I assured her that my time with her was precious and that I looked forward to our next visit together as we still had so much to discuss—like where she had met her husband, how he had proposed, where they had lived or traveled, stories about their children, etc. I let her know that part of our grief journey is sharing our loss with others, but it is in the telling of our lives with our loved one, the smallest and largest of details, that we begin the healing and I wanted to be there through it all—the beginning, the middle and the end.

She looked at me in disbelief at first, but then seemed to warm to the idea that I truly was interested in her story and that I would be back again and again and again—as long as she needed—to talk about her loss. Too many times people forget that when someone dies, if we do not strive to keep their memory alive, their story dies. As a reader and one who thirsts for knowledge, I encourage everyone to share their story—whether you are five, fifty, or one hundred. Everyone has a story to tell and it is in the telling of it that we learn that age is truly just a number.

Don't Rain on My Parade

I saw it happen with my own eyes and I was deeply saddened. While conversing with some individuals, one of their phones lit up and music blared announcing to all that someone was calling. The recipient of the call glanced at the screen, gave a deep sigh, rolled her eyes and hit the ignore button. Curious, I asked if it was one of those pesky telemarketers and she said, "No that was my best friend. Her husband died recently and she calls me all the time and just cries constantly. I'll call her later." She then proceeded to join back in the conversation with the others and made a sarcastic remark about how "some people could just bring your mood down." Inside I was steaming with anger about her flippant attitude towards a friend who was obviously in need of her support, and I bit my tongue to keep from flying off the handle about what I perceived to be her "insensitivity."

Walking back to my car, I reflected on what had just happened and acknowledged that this was not an anomaly. This happens quite often and I hear the proof from those who are grieving as they express the absolute hurt and rejection they feel from friends who seem to distance themselves from them in their time of need. I realize that not everyone is well-versed in grief support and are not aware of how their actions can deeply impact someone's healing, so I work on practicing forgiveness and then implementing subtle education to help people see how they can become more supportive.

In a recent support group, many members shared that this has happened to them—and for some, it happens so frequently they begin to wonder if something is wrong with them. Friendships are tested, broken, and some shattered beyond repair due to lack of communication or understanding. The group asked me to write a column addressing some of these issues so that people will understand that after a death occurs, they are in need of support. When phone calls are avoided or lunch dates are canceled, a clear message is sent to the bereaved that you are unable to be present for them and that is a hurt that goes beyond measure. Remember that grief can create fragility and clouded minds. A simple word or tone of voice can create a sense of bitter rejection that can amplify the pain they are feeling and lead to unnecessary hurt and confusion.

As one member shared, "I have two plants that I used to keep side by side in my house. One day I decided to move one of the plants to the other side of the room to brighten up that corner. After some time, I realized that the plants started to fail—the leaves grew withered and yellow and so I watered them more and paid more attention to their care. When they still were showing no signs of improvement, I decided to move the plants back to their original spot—side by side. Within days, both plants perked up and are now healthy and thriving." Once he shared that with the group, words of amazement and understanding were shared about how perfect an example that was about some of their broken friendships. Their need for comfort and healing, to receive presence and support from their friends was first and foremost on their minds and they craved the attention. Through tears they talked about how they know it cannot be pleasant to always listen to someone who is devastated from loss, but they are hopeful that, with their help, things will get better.

In closing, take a moment to think about the times we may have been guilty of hitting the ignore button, or of dodging an encounter with one of our friends. True, they may be "raining on our parade," putting a damper on our happiness and joy at that moment, but consider the fact that you may be their only umbrella during this storm. By answering that call we demonstrate that we are willing to protect them from the downpour and are ready to walk alongside them in the storm.

Grocery Store Grief

The day started off like any other and she was sincerely surprised when it spun out of control and in how quickly it happened. Her morning jog in the neighborhood was uneventful; her daily breakfast of lightly buttered toast and sliced fruit was simple yet filling. The plan for the day was to make a fast trip to the grocery store, in and out, just a few items, and to return to her "safe place"—her home and garden that awaited her. Clutching the list in her hands, she made her way up and down the aisles collecting what she needed—her mind focused on the task. And then, around the corner, she ran into one of her friends from church. With sudden clarity, she sensed the moment the lady was going to ask her how she was doing and it seemed as if time stood still. Within mere seconds, she found herself crying uncontrollably and watched as her embarassed friend hastily uttered an apology and disappeared almost as quickly as she had arrived. "Clean up on aisle seven," roared overhead and she looked down at the crushed package of eggs now lying on the ground. Feeling as if everyone was staring at her, she abandoned her cart and ran out into the parking lot, shaken by the unexpected events and wondering what had just happened.

Though this may sound extreme to you, it is an experience that is shared by many. Something as simple as going to the grocery store can prove to be filled with anxiety and trepidation, often resulting in forgetting things or leaving the store without purchasing a single item. For others, just looking into their cart and realizing that the number of items they are shopping for has decreased due to the death of their loved one is a difficult reminder that they are now shopping for one. Then, there are the times when we are hopeful that we can run in and out and never see anyone we know, wishing to avoid awkward conversations. No one wants to stand over the cantaloupes and discuss their grief, and yet, if we stood there and talked "shop" and never once spoke about our loss, it might feel as though we were stuck in the frozen food section—cold and unable to express our innermost sadness.

And then there are other people who struggle with loneliness and seek out familiar faces at the grocery store. For them it proves to be a sanctuary of sorts because they know that the clerks will ask how they are doing and at times will share stories of something funny that happened or how they remembered a particular type of pear that their loved one was fond of over the years. This personal touch can be comforting to some and nearly impossible for others to bear. I am reminded of a young woman who had carried her unborn child to term and found several ladies at her local store who were also expecting. They shared in the unbridled joy of awaiting the births of their children and enjoyed checking in on one another throughout their pregnancies. But then the unthinkable happened and the young woman lost her child. For her, perhaps one of the hardest things to do was to go to the grocery store from that point forward because she didn't wish to have to share her grief or talk about the devastating loss of her baby. Having to see her circle of friends with their pictures of the newborns proudly on display, or watch them wheel their children around the store in the buggy was too much to bear, so she drove miles out of her way to shop where no one would know about her situation.

As the friends and family of those who have experienced loss, it is difficult for us to determine how we should react to seeing our friends in public places, such as the grocery store, soon after a loss. Pay attention to their non-verbal cues and to what they are saying or not saying. Let them know that you love them and are there for them—offer to take them out to lunch and follow through on that invitation. The grocery store can be a welcome social event for some, but for others, the task can be stressful and filled with anxiety. "Milk, bread, and eggs," is no longer a quick run to the store for those who are grieving. Allow yourself the opportunity to feel sad and know that there is no shame in "crying over spilt milk." It happens all the time, to many of us, and there is also no shame in "Clean up on aisle seven."

Mailbox Memories

The postman opened the box and placed the mail in the receptacle taking care to notice the numerous cards in the stack. He had observed over the last few weeks that more and more cars had arrived and at first he had found himself perturbed at the ones that blocked his access to the mailbox. Once, he later admitted, he drove off in a huff, refusing to deliver the mail because someone had the gall to park right in front of where he needed to be, blocking his easy access and making his job more difficult. When he went home that night, he recalled this action and chastised himself for being so petty, certain that no one was setting out to impede his job or make his work load any harder.

The next day, as he rounded the corner, he noticed the cars again. But, this time they were lined up for an entire block and he saw people exiting their vehicles carrying containers and dishes full of food. As he pulled up to the mailbox and saw that it was barricaded once more, he made the decision to put his truck in park. Turning on the hazard lights, he lifted the newest stack of mail from his bin and held it thoughtfully in his hand for he now understood what was happening and what all of this mail meant to this family. Stepping out of his truck, he made his way to the front door and rang the bell. He hardly recognized the man who answered the door but he knew it was him. The same man who would wave at him as he drove by while he was in the yard gardening; the same man who would occasionally wait at the side of the road and strike up a conversation about the latest scores of the local ballgames; the same man who would lovingly help his wife out of the car and carry the groceries inside while balancing her on his free arm—it was him, yet he was changed. Gone was the adoring look of love he had for his wife and the carefree glimmer of happiness that would often dance in his eyes. In its place was a look so forlorn and lost that it made him appear as a stranger.

Shakily, he reached out to deliver what he now understood to be condolences for the loss of this man's wife, and found himself crying silently on the doorstep. He knew he was just there to deliver the mail, but he felt a connection to this family. For twenty plus years he had brought to them the latest magazines and packages from far and wide. By delivering their mail, it was almost as if he knew them intimately, as if they were like family, and he was sad. He did not feel right just dropping the cards into the mailbox because he wanted to express to this man that he would miss her, too—the woman who loved to wear hats and sit on the porch and feed the birds.

As if he understood, the grieving man reached out and embraced him and let him know he appreciated him stopping by—that it had meant a lot to him, and he graciously accepted the stack of mail and walked quietly back inside the house. Wiping his eyes, the postman made his way toward his vehicle and took note of all of the visitors still lining the walkways and pulling into spaces that were not normally parking spaces. Without having to look, he knew that every mailbox down the street would be obstructed but instead of being frustrated, he realized he was actually filled with happiness. To know fully how much this sweet woman was loved within her community and by her family made him decide to do something different today. Loading up the mail into a satchel, he locked the truck and began to make his way down the street so that he could deliver the mail in person. Just for today, he wanted to make a personal connection and let his customers know that they were more than just a name on an envelope.

The Never Ending Love Story

He used to be there waiting for me just outside our meeting room. His hair would be disheveled and his clothes a little worn; his gait unsteady as he climbed to his feet to give me a warm greeting. The beat-up truck with all of the stickers on it from years of travel sat in the parking lot and always alerted me to his presence. I looked forward to seeing him. He was a combat veteran that had been involved in heavy fighting in three wars and had received nine bronze stars for his bravery and valor. To me, he was an incredible hero filled with knowledge and insight above and beyond my years, and when he talked, I listened.

In the front pocket of his button-down shirt, he would gingerly remove the black and white picture of his wife, taken the day that they met. His eyes shone with pride as he bragged about her beauty and how lucky he was to have captured her heart. Then, he would drop his eyes, lower his head and begin to let loose a multitude of tears that flowed seemingly without end—tears that symbolized his undying love for his wife.

I remember the first day he extracted that well-worn picture and shared it with the group. It had been roughly nine months since he started attending our meetings and he was always gruff and abrupt, his voice a little too forceful and loud. As a veteran, he prided himself in his stoicism and made it a point to share that "tears were not allowed" and "he was fine" and "didn't need any help." People struggled to understand him at times and even avoided sitting near him for fear that he might speak harshly or belittle something they had to share. In his defense, he was hard to love, however, love him I did. I grew to admire his means of survival—even more so when the battle defenses were swallowed up and his true emotions came rushing forward.

This man described the horrors of war and his share of brutal death scenes and situations. Through it all, he confided that he never shed a tear, but always pushed on in his duty to fight for God and his country. After his wife died, the grief of all those years in combat assaulted him in his dreams and followed him throughout his days.

He struggled to make sense of his role in the deaths of many and the survivor's guilt of having lived when so many of his buddies died—some directly beside him. But through it all, he hung onto the one thing that kept him focused and determined to live, and that was the love he carried for his wife. He treasured her and spoiled her. She provided him with a loving family and years of memories that made him feel honored to have been a husband and a dad. Witnessing the kind of love and devotion he held for his wife impacted me and often left me struggling to breathe. That this man, so hardened by war and so full of defense mechanisms, could break down and be crushed by the loss of his wife humbled me more than I cared to admit.

Never did a meeting pass from that point forward, that he did not extract that picture of his wife—his hands shaking to keep it steady, in order to proudly pass it around. In time, people began to gravitate towards him and encourage him to share his life stories. As he began to process a lifetime of grief and loss, he slowly began to live again and his group embraced him. When he was unable to attend groups due to declining health, I made the drive to his home. He had a small space that he lived in, and the rest, he kept exactly the way his wife had left it. Her wedding dress hung alongside the china cabinet and his walls held countless pictures of their years together. Though he was still living, the past stood still around him, the presence of his wife could be felt around every corner. This was his tribute to her—to their never ending love story. He admitted he was ready to be reunited with her and he smiled when he said that she was "as beautiful the day she died as the day I first laid eyes on her."

Before I left, I thanked him for sharing his love of his wife with me. I told him that I understood how private a man he was and how intimate the gift was that he had given me today. He gave me a kiss on the cheek, a sharp salute and shut the door behind me. As I passed by the window, I saw him sitting on the couch, and I watched with tears in my eyes as he reached into his pocket, placed a soft kiss on the picture of his wife—his most prized possession—then gently tucked it back away.

Remember the Children

"If there ever comes a day when we can't be together,
keep me in your heart, I'll stay there forever."

– A. A. Milne

Remember the Children When Death Occurs

I received a three-page handwritten letter from a mother who poured her heart out to me about the way in which her child had been grieving since the death of her father. What stood out to me the most is that even though it had been years since the death had occurred, the child had recently admitted she had been feeling tremendous guilt about the day her father died. Unbeknownst to her mother, the child had harbored feelings of self-loathing for a reason that may sound silly to us, but in the context of the event, meant everything to the child. What we don't always understand as parents is that children are very complex and are filled with an assortment of emotions that are often difficult for them to identify, let alone express. In this case, the child felt guilty because she had asked to stop at a fast food restaurant for something to eat on the way to the hospital, and when they arrived, her father had just died. They missed it— they weren't there and that is when the seed was planted in this small child that it was "her fault."

This is not an unusual story when children are involved. Many times I have heard about kids who feel like their loved one died because they were bad in school; didn't pray hard enough; or chose to go do something fun on the day of the death and weren't present when they died. Guilt runs rampant through their minds as they wonder what they could have done differently, which often results in sleepless nights and underlying anxiety that can come across as severe irritability or depression. When talking with parents after a death happens, some are very quick to ask questions about how to be supportive of their child, what questions they should ask, and in general, what kinds of signs or symptoms they should be concerned about. Other parents quickly discount grief support and state that their child is fine, that they are doing well and handling things with no problems. Both of these scenarios occur daily and neither is false. Children are resilient and they do cope well in many situations, however, I always try to remind parents that even though outwardly everything may look okay, sometimes we don't know what may be festering inside and it can't hurt to offer support and let them know that there are people available for them to validate their feelings and let them know that they matter.

In the opening example was the case of a mother who was vigilant, present, and encouraged communication, yet it was years before the child was able to identify and vocalize her feelings of guilt and shame. I feel confident that it was because this mother created a safe environment for her child and showed her it was okay to discuss her father that this information finally came to light. Once it was out in the open, the healing could begin as she processed the events from that day. We cannot take away children's feelings and we cannot "fix" their grief, but we can listen and provide moments and opportunities to make things better. For those kids whose feelings have been discounted unintentionally by parents who feel like their kids are "fine and don't need any support," I would ask that they consider revisiting their grief. Not every kid likes to talk about how they are feeling and there are some that will completely shut down when you attempt to get them to do so, however, providing them the opportunity to share and discuss how they have been feeling will go a long way toward their healing.

I have worked with kids and teens of all ages and most have told me that though they are sad and miss the person who died, they really appreciate having someone to talk to about it. For them, just having their feelings validated by someone who let them know they were normal and not alone is all that they needed. Others require more in-depth support and that is fine, too. Nothing is more powerful than watching a child begin to emerge from the depths of despair and find hope again after experiencing a traumatic loss. When I am given the privilege to share their journey, to be present for them along the way, their transformation is clear evidence that grief exists within the bodies and minds of all of us, no matter the age. As parents and caregivers, we owe it to them to acknowledge that their feelings and thoughts matter, and only then can we be satisfied that we have led by example and given them a valid reason to look up to us for support.

Emphasizing Children's Grief Awareness

Just the other day, I overheard a conversation in the hall between several adults that sparked inside of me the need to intervene. The discussion was about a "troubled child," one who had been acting out in class, refusing to do homework and was non-compliant with the rules and regulations meted out by the staff. They were "tired" of having to deal with him and his "attitude" and were desperate for somebody else to take over and address the problem. Unbeknownst to them, this "troubled child" had recently suffered the unexpected death of his older brother who had accidentally overdosed on drugs. The family, too embarrassed to say anything to anyone through fear of the potential stigma, failed to communicate to the school that a significant event had happened within their family. Because of this major communication breakdown, the teen was catapulted into an environment at school where there was lack of understanding for the changes in his behavior, simply because they were unaware. Their indifference and seemingly impossible expectations for this teen, sent him into a tailspin that has taken time to bring under control.

Not surprisingly, this scenario happens more often than not with children/teens who have experienced the death of a loved one. When communication breaks down, so do our children when facing this kind of adversity, and it is up to us to throw them the life preserver that they need—to let them know that we are here for them. What can we do? It is important to remember that children/teens matter. Just because they are not adults, doesn't mean that they could not benefit from having the support of someone who understands grief—someone who is willing to serve as an outlet, as a beacon of hope. Too many times we misunderstand our children's moods and think they are "fine" when really, they are harboring some very deep feelings of anger, anxiety, guilt, or even unresolved sadness that can lead to bouts of depression. Oftentimes, I hear adults state that their kids are "doing fine," which I happen to know is perfectly true in a lot of cases. However, wouldn't it be a good idea to at least give them an opportunity to have some outside support and not assume we know how they are feeling?

Sadness in a Bottle

I want you to think back to a time when you played a practical joke on your sister or brother; a time when you grabbed that ice cold Coca-Cola out of the fridge, shook it up, and handed it to your sibling while you then waited in anticipation of the explosion that was sure to follow. Once that top was popped open, you laughed hysterically while soda fizzed and spewed all over the place, an outburst of pent up energy that was looking to find a place to spread its wings. I'm here to tell you that grief is a lot like that soda in a can. As kids/teenagers, we spend a lot of time holding in our emotions and feelings. We do this for a lot of reasons and here are a few:

(1) Sometimes we truly don't understand what we are feeling
(2) Frequently, we don't know how to identify the feelings we are having
(3) It is often difficult to express how we feel
(4) We try to protect our parent(s) because we don't want them to hurt or be sad
(5) We may just be private and not comfortable sharing our feelings

Looking at the above list, it is almost certain that you fall into one or more of those categories. As kids/teens, it is often instinctual to want to help our parent(s) through their sadness, to protect them from the hurt and pain they are going through. When we do this, we find ourselves internalizing our own feelings, holding them inside where they continue to harbor and fester, waiting for an opportunity to burst forth. The more we hold onto those feelings, the more that we drink them in, swallow them down and keep them inside, the more likely it is that we are heading towards an explosive demonstration of feelings.

Think about this: As you take in more hurt and sadness, it is like someone slowly shaking up your can. The can is only so big and can only handle a small amount of pressure. The more the can is shaken, the more violent that energy becomes and once it has the tiniest opening, well, you know the result. So, in theory, instead of internalizing our feelings, we should be encouraged to find ways to express ourselves in a healthy way. Our parent(s) would want us to share our feelings with them because they are worried about us and vice versa. Wouldn't it be nice for our parent(s) to model for us that it is okay to cry and it is okay to talk about the death and the hurt that we are feeling? We are humans and it is in our nature to be protective of our loved ones. The more we can work on letting some of those feelings out of our can, the healthier our grief journey will be. Let's not wait for the pressure to build to the point where things become explosive—let's share our feelings together and let that sadness out of our can. Maybe then, we can find some relief and truly enjoy having our Coke with a smile.

The Many Ways Children/Teens Grieve

Those who know me are aware of the passion I harbor for what I call "our forgotten mourners." Until recently, the field of child and adolescent grief has been relatively new—brought to the forefront by the unexpected and tragic events of the Oklahoma City Bombing and 9-11. Since then, there has been an onslaught of research and field studies conducted on how to best reach out to our children and support them through their grief journey. And, though there has been much progress, there is still a lot out there that is unknown and a lot left to learn.

One of the most important things we should take note of is that even though children are resilient and can handle most things, that does not mean that they couldn't benefit from having some support. If we make the mistake of assuming that our children are okay because they are children, we may in fact be doing them a massive injustice. Children often take their cues from the adults around them, and in turn mimic behavior that may not be conducive to healing. If they are told to "be strong," or "don't cry," they learn to internalize what they are feeling, stuffing down their grief and thus hiding it away from others. What happens if nobody pays attention to the children and the grief they are concealing is never addressed?

Due to the many different levels of cognitive development, children often have a hard time not only identifying their feelings, but also expressing them. The most important role we have as adults during this time is to be present for our children. By being present, we are letting them know that we are aware of them; we are paying attention to their moods and behaviors; we are giving them permission to communicate. Even if we do all of those things, it still does not ensure us that our children will each receive an "A" on their Grief Journey report card. However, it does go a long way when they are aware they have a safe place to vent and to explore what they are feeling.

When children are ignored, or protected from all things "grief-related," we often see behaviors set in that can become troublesome. For example, it is not uncommon to see escalation in drinking or drug use (often to numb the pain or make them forget), anger and irritability (fighting), lack of motivation, poor school performance, change in appetite or sleep patterns, or other such behaviors. If we notice some of these changes in our child, it should be a red flag to pay attention to, but it does not necessarily mean we should raise an alarm. Just as with adults, *some* of these changes are normal responses and reactions to the loss and are a natural part of grieving. By being present for them, we can approach them with love and understanding. We can assure them that we are paying attention and are eager to hear what is on their mind. Our willingness to include them in the grief journey and our open encouragement is the key to a healthy grieving child. Take time to become more aware of children's grief and their need to be a part of the ritual of healing along with us. Keep in mind that any child old enough to love, is old enough to mourn. We have a responsibility to remember our children when a death occurs—they depend on us to show them the way.

The Unexpected Gift

I don't know many individuals who experience the death of a child who are able to talk about the experience as though it was a gift. I'm not talking about the pretty wrapping paper and bows type of gift and I'm certainly not referring to the joy and excitement felt upon receiving a gift. I'm talking about a beautiful story of a life lived, and one that refers to hope and the promise to "keep on going."

Let me start from the perspective of the adult son who was terminally ill, who bounced back and forth between getting better and crashing more times than a person could count. His attitude about life was simple, "to live it to the fullest." He had a bucket list and I'm not certain how many things he was able to cross off his list—but I do know that he was described as someone who loved life and the people in it, and he wanted to be a positive influence on those around him.

His mother, a diligent worker, found herself being his caregiver—a role she had never anticipated facing. Like all parents, she prayed and hoped that God would heal her child and keep him safe and she remembers the exact moment when she realized that her son was not going to get better—that he was beyond the point of bouncing back, and she wept. The moment was so clear and yet she had many signs along the way that were pointing towards his decline, signs that at the time were not clear or perhaps she simply didn't wish to see or accept. Who wants to accept that death is imminent? Denial helps us make it through each day and it gives us the strength to carry on with our ministering to loved ones. It allows us to put off thinking about the pain and crushing feelings that are soon to assault us. And, it keeps us present in the moment, never wavering from our hope that things will get better and that this situation is different from all others—that they will be healed and be with us forever.

But she knew that her son was tired. He still planted a smile on his face each day and engaged in conversations, appreciative until the end for those who had sacrificed to be present for him, to help him during his time of need. She remembers how he would goad her and encourage her to "go out and live her life, to find love and to engage in living again." Her first instinct was to tell him she *was* living her life, to make excuses for why she hadn't done more for herself, and then she saw the look on his face that told her everything she needed to know. He wanted to be sure that after he died she would not stay stuck in the "pit of despair." He wanted to know that she would engage in living again because she had put her life on hold in so many ways in order to stay at home and take care of him. Most importantly, he reminded her of what she had always told him when he was at a low point—"you can go there, just don't stay."

As she processed all of these things, she understood that he was saying that he could not die until he was certain she was going to be okay; that she would reclaim the life she had paused and push forward even in her grief. He acknowledged that she would be sad and would miss him, but he wanted her to know that she still had a life worth living and that living her life to the fullest would be the best way to honor his death.

Once she understood these things, she crawled into the bed beside him—her boy, always her little boy—and looked into his eyes. She could see the fatigue and feel his need to receive the gift she had yet to give him. Taking a deep breath, she laced her fingers into his, palm to palm and told him that she loved him. She expressed to him that she knew he was tired and then she gave him the biggest gift a mom could ever give—she gave him permission to go. At first his eyes widened in surprise and then he broke out into a smile that lit up the entire room. With a gentle hand squeeze, he conveyed the understanding that she would continue to live, a gift of life that he so desperately wanted her to receive. And with his last breath, he was able to die peacefully, knowing his mother had given him a gift as well, the permission to let go.

The Unbearable Heartbreak of Child Loss

I will never forget the first time I was called down to the emergency room to meet with the mother of a young child who had just died. As I wandered down the hallway trying to imagine what I would encounter when I arrived, nothing could have possibly prepared me for the absolute heartbreak of hearing a parent react to the news that their child is gone. Because it was my first time experiencing child loss, that reaction will always be firmly implanted in my memory. As a counselor, my main focus is on the grieving family, but looking around the ER, it was readily apparent to me that all of the first responders, physicians, nurses, and others, were also greatly affected. Their vacant eyes told me they shared in the loss of this precious child, this life that they tried so desperately to save but could not. Nothing compares to the difficulty of witnessing the death of a child— experiencing it first hand. People will say "it's not natural" or "kids aren't supposed to die before their parents." The sad truth of the matter is that they do, and unfortunately, it happens more than we realize.

What qualifies as a child loss? To those who have experienced child loss, it is often a fragile and sometimes explosive question. Some only consider the death of a child as being a child who was living and breathing outside of the womb. For mothers who suffer the tragedy of a miscarriage or stillborn child, or one who dies shortly after birth, they are often overlooked in terms of their grief journey—many times ignored or made to feel as though they really didn't have anything to grieve because their baby did not live. What is sad to me is that there are actually people who consider there to be different levels of grieving for child loss, and that is simply dumbfounding. No one wants to experience this kind of devastation, and placing any kind of category upon it is simply unfair and misinformed.

Another issue that often occurs is when a grieving parent is asked how many children they have. Of course this is a simple and even common question that comes up in conversation with others. However, when it is asked to someone who has lost a child, the question can cause distress, confusion and sometimes guilt, or some combination of all of those. How do you answer? Do you acknowledge that you have three children—two living and one that has passed? Or, do you say you have two children and not mention that you had another child? Remember that each person is different and how they choose to respond is what is most comforting to them. As a friend or family member, try to be supportive and understanding by having a conversation about how to communicate about the deceased child. This would be a welcome way to possibly avoid uncomfortable situations for both yourself and for the person who is grieving.

Camp Good Grief: The Importance of
Supporting Children

In 2005, I had the privilege of leading a small grief group of fourth and fifth graders at a school, all of whom had experienced the death of a parent over the summer. What was astonishing to me was that none of them were aware of each others' loss because no one was talking about it, and several of them were even in the same class. To witness the feeling of validation that was immediate for them, the instant release of weight upon their shoulders was incredible. If children could leave that setting after having met just once with so much relief, what could happen if we were able to provide something consistent and that reached out to more people?

Enter the idea for Camp Good Grief, the premise being a FREE day camp for children between the ages of five and eighteen who have experienced a death-related loss. After some research, I established a working committee that shared similar views and interests as mine. With a project this large, the workload definitely needed to be shared among many individuals to ensure that this dream would become a reality. Important issues such as: liability and legal issues; a place to hold the function; naming of the camp; the recruitment of volunteers; marketing; identifying needy children; programming; creating registration and distributing forms; parent support etc., were all new to us that first year and had their kinks that needed to be worked out. It was a tall task but one everyone was on board with, and watching it all come together was truly a sight to see.

I have fond memories of all of our camps (at the time of this publishing, we have had twelve), but the first one stands out for many reasons. It was the one that nobody thought we would be able to put together; that no one would attend; and wouldn't be successful. But successful it was, and from that point forward we established ourselves firmly within our community, becomming known as a company that served and supported area children who had experienced a death related loss within a safe and therapeutic setting. The ongoing viewpoint was the simple premise that if we were able to support and help at least one child or their family, then it was worth it.

Over the years we have watched Camp Good Grief grow and develop. It has reached further and further into the community, involving funeral homes, schools, churches and all manner of establishments whose sole purpose is to contribute in a way that best supports of our grieving children. Every year, new people approach me with ideas or visions of how they would like to be involved, and every year I am blown away by the generosity of a community that understands the need to be there for those individuals whose quest for normalcy after experiencing a traumatic event outweighs even the sadness that they feel at times.

Every year we learn something new about ourselves and about how we operate. People, who come by to observe and shadow our camp so that they can start one in their area, are often overwhelmed at first due to the large-scale nature of our camp. However, what I tell them is this—we did not get here overnight. In order to create a supportive environment, the key is to have the ideas, the desire and the support to get your first camp off the ground. Each year you will grow and build on the one before and this is what makes each camp unique. It's about involving your community and having them "buy in." Once you achieve that, you will have planted the seed that will bring forth a harvest full of positive experiences and smiles on the faces of grieving children for years to come.

Violence Creates Complicated Grief

As Twitter exploded with the news that another tragedy had taken place in our community, I prepared myself for the aftermath and wondered about the ones left behind. Everywhere you looked, stories were popping up on TV and social media, and discussions and opinions were discussed as people shook their heads at the senselessness of young lives lost before they were even given a chance to truly live. Every time something like this occurs, you wonder about what could have been, or why things like this have to happen. In short, there are simply no reasonable explanations and no one has the answers as to why arguments turn into shootouts, leaving bloodshed and death-symbols of loss and devastation.

In thinking about these events, my mind wanders to the young children and teens that now have to grieve the loss of a father, mother, sibling, or other relative. I often have held them in my arms as they have cried about the death, but then just as often would scream in anger and confusion as to why this took place in their lives. Because violence played a role, it often brings about a complicated set of emotions that can be difficult to identify and express, especially amongst their peers. For example, how can you explain that you feel sad about the death of your parent when that parent shot and killed somebody else? Or how about the guilt you feel because you still love them and miss them even though they are sitting in prison sentenced to life or death for their actions?

Everyone knows how impressionable children are and how easily they are influenced by their surroundings. Losing a parent or family member is hard, but when death occurs due to a violent action, it can create feelings and behaviors that are difficult to harness-feelings of intense rage or shame; isolation or blame; acting out or seeking out much needed attention. Nobody can blame these children whose ability to process differs based upon their cognitive development and the information given to them. Some families are extremely protective and won't allow honest and accurate information to be given to their children, however it is well known that if the information exists, it will more than likely be discovered. And, if the kids are hearing this information from people outside of their family systems, it can create feelings of mistrust and even betrayal.

Just the other day, I listened as a young girl talked about how much her life had changed as a result of the actions taken by her father. Because he killed someone, and in this instance it was another family member, he is now in prison awaiting sentencing. For her, the losses she presently faces are too numerous to count, but are every bit as impactful. She has had to move, start another school, make new friends, and mourn the loss of her family member who died-all while trying to process her father's actions and juggle feelings she has that change constantly. One minute she is angry—the next, she is crying her eyes out at all that she has lost. All too often, people tend to focus more on the actual death of a person and not look at all of the secondary losses that can cause complications in children who are still trying to figure out their own feelings and emotions at such a sensitive time in their lives. No better example can be given than the time I asked a child to draw how he was feeling on a piece of paper, and after several minutes, he picked up the crayons and scribbled furiously all over the page, carefully writing at the top, "mixed emotions."

Upon seeing that display of feelings and the absolute confusion he was experiencing, it clearly demonstrated how difficult it can be for kids and teens to navigate through their grief journey, especially when the death involves violence or leaves behind questions that require further answers. So, for us—the family, friends, teachers, counselors, and support systems, it is important to remember that death has many layers. A child who is acting out is not a "problem child," but instead may have experienced significant loss that has influenced his/her behaviors and actions. Try to think outside the box; gather them into your arms when able; go the extra mile to reach out to them and break down their walls. When we show them that we care, the power of healing takes on a whole new meaning and we are more likely to see significant growth and change in a positive direction. Violence may cause the loss of life, but the ones left behind still need to find the hope that gives them a reason to keep living.

Living and Grieving

"I know for certain that we never lose the people we love, even to death. They continue to participate in every act, thought and decision we make. Their love leaves an indelible imprint in our memories. We find comfort in knowing that our lives have been enriched by having shared their love."

– Leo Buscaglia

A "Cuppa Mourning" Joe

He trudged into the kitchen, turning on lights as he went, pressing the start button on the ever faithful percolator. Cabinets opened and closed as he prepared his morning breakfast, his appetite so poor he wanted nothing more than a piece of toast. With slippers on, he walked to the end of the driveway to snag the morning edition and placed it on the table beside her chair. She loved the funnies and would giggle innocently, a sweet smile upon her face as she reached across him and pointed out a particular one she wanted him to peruse. If he tried really hard, he could close his eyes and almost hear that beautiful sound—the sound of her laughter and the way she ruffled the paper to get his attention. But most mornings, even though he gave an extra effort, the sound of her voice seemed to be fading along with the memories of their times spent together at this kitchen table.

With a sigh, his trembling hand picked up his favorite coffee mug and transferred his portion into her cup. For him, placing his lips along the rim of her battered mug made him feel a closeness to her that he craved almost as much as the caffeine that he ingested. Though it had been months since her death, he still found himself setting the table for two—the act of not doing so seemed unbearable and foreign, and besides it brought him comfort to imagine her sitting there with him. Sleep did not come easy which made the nights long, but the morning routine was perhaps the hardest. Never had they missed a morning meal together and the simple ritual of sipping coffee in silence and reading their daily devotional was a special bond between them.

Finishing his coffee, he shook his head at the absolute loss that he felt. Friends told him that things would get better, if he just stayed busy, time would heal everything. Though he knew these things, he suffered in silence and berated himself for not being able to start each day with a little more bounce in his step. Mornings were crushing because he felt the loss of her more intensely than at any other time of the day. In his grief, he felt stuck, unable to avoid starting off each day feeling sad and alone. He secretly wished he could sleep until noon each day and skip breakfast altogether. Then, he would chide himself for the thought of betraying something so dear to him. Even though it hurt terribly, it was also the moment when he felt the closest to her and that was something that he would never let go—pain or no pain.

He pondered the two mugs before him—mugs they had both settled upon over the years, each claiming one over the other. He lovingly caressed the chipped handle of her mug, remembering how it had happened and how upset she had been. But then, she smiled at him and talked about how it gave it character. That was the way it was between them—so simple and giving—a routine filled with nourishment and love that always seemed to start their day off on the right foot. Now he struggled to find that comfort and her empty chair signaled her absence, making it difficult for him to breathe.

Reverently, he went to the sink and washed out their cups, setting them side-by-side on the window sill—the paint there a slightly different shade from where they rested over years in the sun. His spot and hers, together forming a whole, the way it was supposed to be. Turning away from the window, he grabbed the comics and settled down into his favorite chair. With the smell of coffee still lingering in the room, he smiled at the memory of her laughter, and recognized that the simple memory of all of these things was the best part of waking up.

Answers to a Father's Prayers

As he sat across from me, the story began to unfold in leaps and bounds. The recent death of his daughter had served a blow to him that left him feeling lost and uncertain and he wondered how he could ever begin moving forward. As an engineer and a home builder, he was looking at grief as being just another "problem to solve." After much time spent in vain trying to discover the solution, he realized that this problem was unsolvable, and his despair had woven itself across his face and settled into his eyes. What happened the next time we met was something he wished to share with others and so at his request, I share with you a message about hope and the power of answered prayers.

There is an old adage often repeated after the death of a loved one—"everything happens for a reason." For those who are grieving, this is in no way comforting to them. This statement often fuels anger as well as disbelief that someone could say something so callous during a time of loss. However, there are also those who are able to look at events and see them as signs that appear to be sending a message. If they are in the right frame of mind, they can receive the message and see how many things had to happen in order for the message to be discovered. They can then look back and realize how "God's work" had to be involved.

This father had entered the doctor's office with a loved one and had taken a seat. Initially, he hadn't planned on accompanying her on this visit but at the last minute decided to go along. The doctor's office was in another state and the reception area was filled with out-of-date magazines. Reaching over to one of the tables, he picked up an issue of *TIME* and realizing it was current, he settled in to read about the death of Nancy Reagan. As he flipped through the pages, he found himself drawn to the picture of the former first lady as she was draped over her husband's casket—unwilling to leave his side. Overcome with emotion, he quickly closed the magazine and set it aside, his feelings too raw to read any further. But something drew him back and he found himself again reading about one of America's greatest love stories. Once again, he closed the magazine and put it down only to find himself feeling drawn to pick it up one more time. His mouth went dry as he read the paragraph about Nancy asking Billy Graham, the spiritual leader, for reassurance that her husband was in heaven. Reverand Graham simply responded, "Oh, yes."

The man felt a sudden lift in his spirit from these words as he recalled his daughter, a few days before she died, telling him that she was ready to be with her Lord, and she knew where she was going. He had needed his own reassurance and here, in this doctor's office, he felt like he had been given the answer he so desperately needed. Then, he looked at all the events that had to transpire in order to receive this message: the decision to accompany a loved one to the doctor; the fact that it was across state lines; how he could have chosen anywhere to sit and might never have seen that particular magazine; how he picked it up and put it down three times; and how Nancy's death just happened one day before his daughter's.

Overcome with emotion while sharing his story, the man stated that experiencing something as powerful as this had altered his grief path in a positive way. Yes, he is still struggling and knows that will be the case for a while, but having received what he perceived to be a "message, loud and clear" was an answer to a prayer that would help him move forward in the direction of solving the elusive problem of healing.

Heaven is for Pets, Too

For those of you who have never experienced the wonders and joys of having a pet, you probably aren't able to understand what it feels like to lose one. Over the years, I have held many a grief support session for those who have experienced this pain, and some of the bereaved have made statements like, "I know it sounds weird, but losing my dog/cat has been harder on me than losing a family member." With that said, I know some of you are scoffing or shaking your head and thinking, *that* is some kind of "messed up." But, it is absolutely true that the bond we form with our pets is strong and their deaths leave us feeling extreme emptiness and hurt unlike any other.

A year ago, my family was faced with the task of putting two of our babies "to sleep." The anguish over watching their decline and ultimately deciding their fate was extremely hard to bear. We wondered if we were making the right decision and at times, found ourselves using prayer for guidance, seeking permission to do what we knew needed to be done. Silently, I looked into their eyes and begged them to tell me that "it would be okay." I wanted assurance that they were hurting and were ready to go. I needed validation that I was making the best decision for them and that it wasn't about me and what I wanted or needed. Being present at their death, holding them and comforting them as the light slowly dimmed from their eyes was a moment I will never, ever forget. However, I would like to say that it was also a privilege to be there for them, to let them know how much they meant to me and to our family and to let them know that they were not alone.

The grief we feel over the death of our pets is debilitating at times. It can affect our appetite and our sleep patterns; we may not wish to be social, we may wander around in a daze and have difficulty focusing on our job. Tears pop up unexpectedly as we come home and are faced with the hard truth that they are not running to the door to greet us, or not sitting in the window barking at every squirrel or neighbor passing by. Their food dish sits empty, a lost or forgotten toy lies haphazardly in the yard, and that well-worn leash hangs forlornly beside our keys. Nothing can take away the hurt and nothing can fill the gaping hole that has emerged in the absence of their frolicking and chatter.

Sometimes it seems unfair that we are only blessed to have our pets for a minimal amount of time—their life spans are short and over way too soon. But, during those few short years, the memories pile up and we are reminded of the one thing that pets give us that is hard to duplicate—unconditional love. No matter how long we are gone from home, or how harsh our words are at a scolding for an accident or a chewed up shoe, they are always willing to give our face a quick wash with kisses, their tails wagging vigorously with happiness. Many people ask me if I think they will see their pet again after they die. Of course, I have no way of knowing for sure, but in my heart I know that these four-legged members of our family will most definitely be waiting for us when it is our day to enter heaven. And, their eyes will be dancing with light and recognition once again—because they knew we were coming and they wanted to be the first one there to welcome us home.

Animals: Grief and Unconditional Love

Walking down the hall, he felt his heart rate speed up. Something about this building, this place, unnerved him and made the hairs stand up on his neck. Unfamiliar smells assaulted his nose around every turn and because of his scheduled meeting, he did not have the time to stop and explore what they where or where they might be coming from. As he loped along, he felt the strongest desire to stop and stand beside a single door. His family turned back and looked at him, imploring him to hurry along—they were not yet at their destination. But, shaking his head, he felt called to whatever or whomever was on the other side of the door and he began to make a keening noise. Concerned, his family came and attempted to comfort him, but nothing was going to make him move any further.

A noise to his left alerted him that someone else was coming down the hall toward him. A nurse glanced at him briefly, smiled and brushed past him into the room—the door whooshing shut behind her. The tug to go in was tremendous and yet his family was insistent that he join them. Reluctantly, he turned away from the door and made his way toward the person he had been yearning for over the last couple of days. All at once, she spotted him, her eyes filled with joy and unspoken love and she held her arms out for him to join her. With a leap, he was up on the bed and lathering her with sloppy kisses, happy to be reunited with his human mom. She laughed at his "puppy-like" excitement and moved over to make room for him on the bed. And just like that, a family was reunited.

Next door, people rushed in and out of the room and he sensed that something had changed. Earlier, he had felt the need to be very still, to stand vigil at that door. Now he knew that the person inside of that room was gone and it made him sad. Inching closer to his mom, he implored her to look at him and assure him that she was going to be with him forever—that she was not going to leave him. He knew something had happened recently and it made his stomach queasy. His food bowl remained full, his toys still in their basket because he couldn't understand where she had gone. Wandering around the house looking for her and waiting on the back of the sofa staring forlornly out the window did nothing to bring her back. But someone thought to stop by the house and bring him here—to this place. And he was happy. Being with his mom comforted him and allowed him to relax enough to drift off into a light sleep, her heart beating steadily alongside his own.

To this day, he doesn't remember if it was the sound of someone crying, or the absence of the warmth beside him that caused him to wake. He felt gentle, caring hands reach down and attempt to move him from her side but he wedged himself in closer. Somewhere deep within, he felt the music of his soul as it drifted up and out, his mourning song filling the room with his sadness. Memories flashed before his eyes—the day she first laid eyes on him at the animal shelter; the car rides in the country; ice cream cone treats after the vet; and his most precious memory, the nighttime ritual of lying beside her, safe and warm. What was going to happen now? Did he have to go back to the shelter? Who would love him?

Panic set in as he looked around the room at all of the people who loved his mom as much as he did. His eyes settled on her best friend, the one who came by for coffee every morning and always patted him on the head with affection. Through her tears, she smiled at him and lifted up his walking leash in her hands. His heart, though broken in pieces, soared briefly as he realized that he was still loved and that he would have a home. Nuzzling in once more to the first mom who rescued him, he took a moment to inhale the wondrous beauty of her scent, memorized it and then quietly hopped down off the bed. As he made his way over to the woman across the room, he watched her drop down to her knees and he felt joy as he was wrapped into her loving arms.

A Breath of Fresh Air

When I walked into her room, she attempted to sit up and then collapsed back onto the bed from exhaustion. Her eyes signaled that something had changed from the last time we had met, as she smiled at me, patted the side of her bed and invited me to come closer. With no hesitation, I reached out for her hand and leaned in to hear the words she was speaking—her breath labored, her voice soft as a whisper. It was at this moment that she said to me, "I'm ready." At first, I wanted to argue, to deny, to say that she was being silly—that there was so much time left. But I didn't. I knew that this was her journey, it was not about me. My only choice at this moment was to be attentive and present.

People say all the time that those who are dying give us absolute proof that they know the most about living. Think about that. Those who are faced with their own mortality have the time to contemplate the meaning of life and their approaching death, so they often become teachers for those of us who are being left behind. The problem lies in the fact that most of us, as students, are unwilling to listen and learn what it is they have to teach us because we are so intently focused on making sure that they keep on living.

At this moment though, I understood what she meant by "being ready," and I acknowledged her statement with a question of my own—"Are you afraid?" Her eyes appeared to dance with light as she answered emphatically, "No. I am not afraid of dying, but then again, I've never died before." I couldn't help but smile at her sense of humor and her courage, and then I wondered how it was that she had reached this point of acceptance. My wait didn't last long as she broke the comfortable silence between us. She said, "I want to be aware of being absent from my body, my last breath escaping me. I want to feel myself transitioning from this world into the glorious presence of my Lord." The absolute calm that she exuded was one of peace and longing. Her daily work towards this moment in her life had led her to the belief that "we are only born once and we only die once" and that it would be an experience she wanted to be an active participant in. Who could fault that type of reasoning?

Even though I have sat bedside at many deaths and have had conversations with individuals about their approaching death, it is very rare to find someone who has settled everything in their minds and who gives off such a strong feeling of acceptance. Honestly, most of the time I am having conversations about anger, denial, fears, "not fairs" and regrets. That is part of processing the end of life—coming to terms with our limited time and becoming more aware of the fact that we are dying and wondering what it will be like. Oftentimes, nerves are ramped up, anxiety is evident and much time is spent meeting with spiritual advisors trying to soothe the possible stains on our human soul. We look for forgiveness and acceptance, acknowledge our faults and generally work on cleansing—all in preparation for the final moment, whenever that may come.

But with this sweet lady—she had already reached this point in her mind and she wanted to make sure that I understood she was fully ready to embrace her death and move toward the next stage—life after death. A spirit that was not afraid, an individual who had accomplished much, yet she was eager to close out this chapter. She told me she felt like she only had a day or two left here and she planned on making the best of it. I glanced around her room, at the pictures on the walls and her journal filled with notes and well wishes. When my eyes settled back on her, I leaned even closer and let her know how precious she was, that she was truly a gift to me and that she was perhaps one of the greatest teachers I had ever known. And believe me . . . I took notes.

Tattered, Torn and Forlorn

She looks at me with some of the saddest eyes I have ever seen and then gently reaches up and touches my face, pulling me closer. Her lips press against my forehead and she whispers her gratitude in my ear as she pulls away. This woman, close to turning a century old, was thanking me for being present for her when she felt as if everyone else had abandoned her a long time ago. In reality, her family does see about her—but, not without making her feel like she is a bother to them. So she tends to sit alone for days by herself—the only human contact being from the care center down the road who delivers her meals.

During our visits, she likes to share memories of her early childhood, especially the ones that left an impact on history. On paper, she pours over notes that she has scribbled down as thoughts and stories come to her mind, forgotten for years but now more vivid and amazing in their telling. What really disturbs me as I sit and listen is how honest she is when she verbalizes how alone she feels and how she cannot understand what she could have possibly done in her life to be "thrown away." Taking her hand in mine, I sense the desperation as she begs me to stay for lunch, that she would be more than happy to "fix me a sandwich," all because she doesn't wish for me to leave. The clock ticks loudly as time passes and I see her calendar on the table—empty of appointments and visits except for a trip to the local beauty parlor later in the month. My heart trembles as I feel myself becoming teary, wondering how in the world someone as precious as this could live this long and yet feel so alone and abandoned just when she needs human contact and kindness the most.

The message she wishes me to convey in this story is that "old people are wonderful and they have a lot to contribute." She talks about how difficult it is to feel like a burden on her family and how she has often struggled when sick, determined to help herself just so she wouldn't have to "bother anyone." What she really wants to convey is that our culture has forgotten what it means to care for our loved ones. "Not all of us," she is quick to say, "but most people have just gotten too busy and tend to forget about the ones who are weak and weary and can no longer do for themselves." In her case, she is one of the lucky ones. Because of expert money management and relatively good health, she has managed to stay in her home where she feels safe and comfortable. The downside to that is because she cannot drive and most of her friends have already died, there is no one left to visit or have phone conversations with any longer.

On one of our visits, the phone rang and I saw her eyes light up with joy as she answered. After a few minutes of animated discussion, the conversation ended and she proceeded to tell me that it was the pharmacy calling about her medication refills. Again, I felt myself saddened because in that moment I could tell how alone she truly felt—she looked forward to even the smallest of interactions. I thought about my own daily encounters and felt momentarily ashamed that I had so many. But then, I realized that I am blessed at this time in my life to recognize the need to be present for others and how engaging in this act of mindfulness, pays me back tenfold.

How can we become more impactful in our community and how can we reach the elderly who are unable to leave their homes or who are residing in facilities behind locked or closed doors. My solution at this time is to write about it; to bring the matter to the attention of all those who are reading; to attempt to plead for a call of action. By doing this, I am hopeful that we will take the time to think about our daily blessings and try to reach out to those who are feeling tattered, torn, forlorn and simply thrown away. These people are treasures and by finding them and being present for them, we will become all the richer.

Regrets are Hard to Forget

Her hands were visibly shaking from the years of choices she had made that had greatly affected her body. Just a few months clean after twenty years of partaking in heavy street drugs—a life that had consumed her—she sat before me with regret. Her mother was dying and after all of the time away, she didn't know what to say to her or how to even begin to apologize for her past mistakes. She was angry and consumed with guilt, so instead of being present for her mother, she found herself avoiding conversations and dancing around topics that had been festering for years.

To begin, I asked her to be honest—not just with me, but with herself. I talked with her about being her "authentic self," and that unless she believed in who she was today, no one else would either. At first, she stared blankly at me, the confusion evident and profound. But then, it was like a fire ignited within her and she started talking about her journey and all the steps she had taken to reach this point in her life. The part that made her the saddest was acknowledging the fact that now, when she had finally made it, her mother was dying and wouldn't be here to see all of the hard work she was doing to rejoin the living, to take her life back from the clutches of drugs.

Her nose twitched, her eyes blinked rapidly and her leg bounced up and down in a constant rhythm that denoted her anxiety and discomfort. Words started to spill out, followed by racking sobs that swallowed her voice making it difficult to understand her story. And it was quite a story—one filled with abuse, living on the street, broken and residing in filth and squalor. Because of the drugs, she lost custody of her children and to this day does not know where they are. She can only hope that someone has given them a better life than she would have provided. Her story was full of one loss after another and her anguish about now having to face the one loss she had not expected to face, the loss of her mother, was quickly approaching.

During our conversation she spoke about her mother's anger toward her and she couldn't understand why she was lashing out.

"Can't she see that I am clean now and that I am here to take care of her?" she asked. She verbalized the hurt she felt and wondered aloud why, when her mother needed her the most, she was pushing her away. Gently, I looked her in the eye and practiced some brutal honesty. I spoke with her about all of those years that her mother was her fiercest champion, the one person who refused to give up on her even after she had burned the bridges in fabulous fashion with all the rest of her friends and family. And yet, she had pushed her mother away, refused her help, and chose instead to worship the drugs that were destroying her life. I mentioned how a mother's love is often unconditional, but that doesn't mean there isn't hurt, regret, and defense mechanisms built up in order to prevent herself from being hurt once again.

Understanding started to cross her face as she recognized that mom was lashing out at her, not for being here now, but because she had been absent for so long—and now she was dying. Questions poured out wondering what she needed to do to "fix this" or how she could express to her mother how sorry she was for disappointing her. Sometimes, the act of being present for someone involves the simple art of listening and gentle guidance—not providing them with all of the answers but allowing them to discover them on their own. In this case, because she was determined to live a better life and not continue to be defined by her past, she made the decision to approach her mother and have the conversations that needed to happen. It was not easy—in fact it was filled with a pain so splitting that she felt like she had been ripped apart—but it was productive. I observed the moment when the last twenty years slowly disappeared as regrets were spoken, tears were spilled, and a mother held her daughter, the prodigal daughter, in her arms of forgiveness.

A Fistful of Obits

I remember as a small child sitting at the kitchen table with my grandmother, devouring my breakfast while she perused the newspaper. The thing that always stood out to me was how she navigated the paper and what she chose to read first (the obituaries) and what she always ended with (the comics). At the time, I remember feeling so sad that she spent part of every morning scanning the obituaries and reading over the stories of the lives who had been lost and seeing how many of them she knew. Carefully, she would make notes of a church member and when their service would be, or a neighborhood friend that would no longer be attending their bridge club.

I watched in silence, not understanding why someone would want to begin their day with something that was so sad—but it was what she did and how she lived her life. When she was ready, I would hand over to her the comics, the bright funnies standing out next to the clippings of the black and white images of the people who had died. She would slowly read over her favorites, chuckle out loud at a line or two, gently fold up the paper and dig into her grapefruit. Now, as an adult—I get it. What I clearly saw no purpose in engaging in as a child, a teenager, and even as a young adult, I now find myself doing. My day starts with scanning those obituaries—what I am looking for, I am not sure that I even know. But, I do know that I take the time to recognize the lives, note the day they were born, the age at which they died and I scan the list of family to see if there is anyone I recognize that I can offer comfort to in their grieving.

What was a practice I first learned about at an early age but adamantly refused to engage in because I thought it was "morbid" and "weird," I am now incorporating into my daily routine. Death is a daily occurrence and it is anything but routine, but now I have the understanding of why it is important to recognize each and every life that leaves this world, even if it is just a moment of reading about their passing.

Interestingly enough, after taking an extended vacation, I walked into the room of a sweet friend of mine who has been diagnosed with a terminal illness. She has understood for months now that her time is limited and she still spends her days trying to focus on others; still laughing and working effortlessly to bring a smile to the faces of those around her. When I sat down and the room became still and quiet, she reached into the bedside table and after some fumbling around, managed to withdraw a fistful of obituaries that she had clipped from the papers and had been saving. Almost reverently, she unfolded them one by one and shared with me more in-depth details about their lives—how one lady had been a friend from high school, another a distant cousin. She talked about their stories and made each one of them come to life for me. Then she grew quiet again and I knew she was wondering why in the world she was still here. I glanced down at that pile of death notices and felt my heart seize with sadness at all of the loss of life, but particularly, the loss of the lives that had impacted this sweet lady over the years.

To live your life surrounded by friends and family; to be impactful in a world that needs service and understanding; to take an active role in living—that is how she had lived her life. And, even though it is well known that not everything is "black and white," and that death comes to us whether or not we are ready, the faces staring at me from all of those clippings spoke loud and clear. Every life matters and that is a headline that should be written boldly and in stone.

A Way Forward

"Loss is nothing else but change,
and change is Nature's delight."

–Marcus Aurelius

Reflections on Dating After the Death of a Loved One

He sat in a well-worn recliner across the room from me with tears in his eyes, hesitant to ask the question—but with encouragement, he did so. "When is it too soon to start dating again?" At that moment, I saw the unbridled pain and anguish of having just lost his wife not two weeks before, and yet, his mind was already jumping toward finding someone else to share his life with. "The loneliness," he explained, "is something that I just don't think I can live with. I want someone to be here when I come home, someone to travel with, someone to listen to me when I need to talk." It was apparent to me that his grief was too heavy to truly be ready to move on to dating, so I gently encouraged him to talk about his loss, along with his long term goals, wants and needs. And, within every bit of that conversation, the dominating factor was being alone and how scary that can be.

Everyone is different. There are some individuals who are fully content in living out the rest of their lives without ever entertaining the thought of meeting someone else or dating. Then, there are those who recognize that they are on a grief journey, and during that journey, time begins to heal and we start to yearn for company—for the healing touch of loving someone again. I have seen those who are quick to jump into the dating scene, convinced that they are ready and have grieved enough. None of these categories of people are right or wrong, because our grief is a journey and it shifts and changes almost daily. One moment, we are adamant that we will never marry again; and then the next day we are startled when someone catches our interest and there is a sweet tug of feelings that had been dormant for a long time.

For those who move on quickly, some of the challenges they may face include: judgment and gossip from society; not being able to fully be present in the current relationship because there is still so much grief and healing going on; guilt because they feel they are dishonoring their deceased loved one; and lastly, when a new relationship falls apart, the complete and utter despair of having to face yet another loss.

Many times, the newly bereaved share with me about the pain and astonishment they feel when people ask them if they are going to get married again, or if they would like to go out on a date. They feel very fragile and vulnerable and sometimes anger sets in because they feel that they are being taken advantage of while facing some of the most difficult times in their lives. What I often say in support counseling to them is this: "Go with your heart. You will know when you are ready, and stop listening to what others think is right for you. If you have been blessed with another opportunity to live the remainder of your life with someone that lifts your spirit, take tentative steps and see where it may lead." There is the old saying, "No pain no gain," and sometimes this definitely rings true when you are navigating the waves of your grief journey.

By the same token, if you are content and are simply not interested in dating or remarriage, that is your prerogative and your decision. Don't fall prey to societal pressure to "fill that space" with someone new. Again, grief is very complicated and the time involved in the process is different for everyone. Whether the idea of moving forward into a new relationship is now, next year, or never—it is up to you. Sometimes blessings and opportunities are quietly waiting for us to reach the right moment and will arrive just when we need them the most.

False Starts After Broken Hearts

There he was, dog leash in hand, walking with his head down along a quiet road. Instinctively, I pulled over to the side of the road because I knew his grief journey and had not seen him in some time since his wife had died. His eyes lit up when he recognized my face as I powered down the window and offered him a smile and a hug, followed quickly with the question foremost on my mind—"How have you been doing?" He chuckled softly, picking his dog up to investigate who had taken away some of his attention, and replied, "You never told me that trying to get back out into the dating world would be so crazy!" This response initiated a conversation that I have had with many others and it made me think about all of the indecisiveness experienced by those who are grieving. I wanted to explore it a little more. His honesty about his experiences thus far and his yearning for companionship to combat the utter loneliness that he constantly faced rang true. Most importantly, the love of his wife was still evident in his trials and tribulations and my heart hurt not only for him, but for many like him that, while grieving, often find themselves on a quest of learning how to live again.

During one support group, a member spoke about how she recognized that while overtures had been made by single men looking for a date, she simply wasn't interested. She said, "I realized that I will always be married to a dead man, and for me, that brings me comfort and peace." Others were clear that their intentions were to find someone else with whom to share the remainder of their life—being alone was not for them. They were frustrated about the dilemma often faced when going out to lunch or coffee, of laughing and finding joy with someone but then feeling overwhelmingly guilty or consumed with what they felt was "disrespect toward their deceased loved one for moving on."

Some recognize that "getting back into the saddle" and looking for love can be filled with many false starts. When grief has become our journey, we often look to fill those empty spaces to combat our sadness and are quick to "try to move on" even if at times we realize we are not ready. What I often tell people is that there is no shame in looking for love or in wanting to share your life with someone. Society often dictates certain rules and regulations as to how this should or should not happen and that can be both hurtful and confusing for those who are simply trying to heal. I know of one gentleman who found someone who made him happy after his wife died. When his minister discovered what was going on, he took him aside and told him that he should no longer have any contact with this lady and used religion to mandate that he take six months to study and participate in grief sharing before he could even consider "moving on." My question to the minister would be, "Who has the right to tell us how we should live our lives and when we *are* or are *not* ready to pursue happiness?"

Many others discover that they are not ready to take the next step soon after dating begins. The constant back and forth of experiences with someone new makes it clear that this person "isn't like my husband or wife" and makes it clear that we are comparing and contrasting. This is a normal part of moving forward but it can be difficult and painful. Our desire to awaken new beginnings brings us to step up time and time again to the starting blocks to give it our best effort. However, as with many races a contestant may be disqualified for jumping the gun and leaving the blocks too soon. We must recognize that the most important part of any race is to continue to push forward. Even if we do not come in first place, finishing the race is the most important thing.

The Lonely Hearts' Club

One by one, they filed into the room, taking note of the other participants. Those who knew each other nodded their hellos and then took a seat while those who entered for the first time appeared to waver at the front door—uncertain of how to proceed. I noticed the fleeting sense of doubt as it crossed their minds. I knew they were conflicted as to whether or not they had made the right choice by coming here, and I quickly offered them a smile and said, "Welcome. I am glad that you are here." For those who remembered their first time, I watched in appreciation as they took on the role of mentor and did their best to make sure a comfort zone was created—though they, too, were grieving and here for healing. Having the opportunity to witness scenes such as these, to see firsthand the power of group healing, is a wonderful experience and it is why the healing efforts of group support goes a long way in an individual grief journey.

No one volunteers to become a member of a grief group. We don't rush to be first in line and in fact many of us resent the fact that our journey has even led us to this time and place in our lives. However, becoming a member of a support group can perhaps be one of the biggest advantages you may have over others in advancing in life simply because you have gained the support of others who are walking a similar path. Why is the group experience so helpful and what can others do for you that you cannot do for yourself? Let's take a look as I am hopeful that by learning more about the group process you will consider giving it a try, thus giving yourself every opportunity to become the best you that you can be.

First, let's start with the words that create the most uncertainty, discomfort and oftentimes fear for those who are grieving: *counselor* and *support group*. *Counselor* tends to elicit thoughts of weakness and the ever popular "there's nothing wrong with me" responses. Traditionally, people think that by speaking to a counselor it means they are unable to cope and it threatens their idea of strength. By entertaining the thought of attending a *support group*, this further demonstrates that they are unable to handle things on their own and creates additional thoughts of failure and fear of what others might think of them. In reality, grief support should be viewed as "support counseling"—an opportunity to allow yourself the freedom to share thoughts and feelings within a therapeutic setting—one that is safe from judgment and one that is filled with the incredible potential of satisfying the need for validation.

Many come to a group for the first time scared out of their minds, but most wind up leaving feeling uplifted and supported. There is something awe-inspiring to witness individuals enter a room with many defense mechanisms in place and watch as one by one they slowly disintegrate into the arms of fellow group members waiting to catch them. Bonds are forged, new relationships are established, and almost everyone leaves with an feeling that they belong. Remember, no one desires to become a member of a group such as this, but while we are on a grief path, why not take advantage of every opportunity to help us further our journey in a positive way?

What many don't understand is that a grief support group can run the gamut of feelings that include sadness, anger, and yes, even uncontrollable laughter. Sometimes we laugh so hard at our own responses and experiences that the sense of relief washing over the room is heartfelt and tremendous to see as it unfolds. Nothing provides more validation than to hear others say, "I thought I was the only one" or to see heads nod in acceptance of something just shared because they have also been there. The feeling of suffering alone disappears almost immediately when surrounded by those who can empathize because they have been there. One member put it so perfectly when he said, "You know, it amazes me that after all this time, there is always something new that I learn by coming here. The drive home is filled with our conversations and gives me food for thought until we meet again."

If you are grieving—first of all, my apologies for your loss and for your pain and suffering. I would like to personally invite you to attend our support group or any group that makes you feel welcomed and encouraged. You have the right to carry the torch of your loss alone, but why choose that path when there are others who can help assist you along the way? Support groups are filled with lonely hearts, but it is a club whose price of admission is the sacrifice that has brought you all together.

The Power of Empathy

Too many times, people rush about from place to place tasked with trying to keep up with the routine worries of their daily lives. We tend to focus on what we have and what we need, rarely taking the time to think about our blessings and the gifts that have been bestowed upon us. This morning, I took part in an empathy exercise with a small group of people and it was life changing.

We were all asked to list five items that we have that are important to us (like a home or a vehicle), five people who are important to us, five abilities of our body that are important (like breathing or talking), five hobbies, and finally five hopes and dreams for our future. Once this was completed, we were then told that we had just received a terminal diagnosis and had only months to live. Instructions were given to then reach into our bags and withdraw six of those items of importance, read them, and then say goodbye to them because they were lost to us forever. After a period of silence, we were instructed to do the same thing again—another six pieces of paper. I realized that in this short period of time, with the removal of just twelve slips of paper, I had now lost the ability to breathe on my own, communicate with others, and had lost both of my parents. I found myself more and more anxious with each unraveling, hoping it wasn't going to be someone else I loved, and then I would relax considerably as one of my material possessions was revealed. But then, the instruction for six more pieces of paper to be removed and everything in my heart shattered as I had to say goodbye to all of my loved ones and all of my independence. The only piece of paper left in my bag of hopes and dreams was "to be successful in life." My hands shook as I looked around at the pile of items that were the most meaningful to me and thought about how unimportant my one remaining item truly was in the grand scheme of life. I was devastated. What was being successful worth if I didn't have anyone to share it with, or couldn't even remember it?

What this exercise teaches us is that we need to be mindful of our friends and family who are currently facing a terminal diagnosis. The things that used to be of utmost importance to them, no longer matter, and sometimes the only thing that keeps them fighting to live another day is the love they hold for their family. As caregivers, friends or family, it is important to remember that there is so much more going on with our dying loved ones, beyond the terminal diagnosis. In their frame of mind, they are losing little pieces of themselves all along the way, with some items disappearing faster than others.

I would encourage us all to be mindful of what it would be like to have to depend on someone else to help us walk to the bathroom, or have faith in a machine to give us oxygen to breathe. We should be aware of the need for patience and understanding as our loved ones struggle to communicate or lose the ability to feed themselves. Showing empathy is difficult because we are simply not in their shoes; we are not walking their path, but are traveling beside them. Awareness is the key to so many things, but in the case of our loved ones who are losing so much every day as they approach death, it is the most important part of the journey. Our empathy and understanding can make all the difference in the world to someone who depends on us, for it is this understanding that translates our love.

Time is Precious

Glancing at the clock on the wall, I realized that my morning was slipping by faster than I had anticipated. I started to have heart palpitations from the anxiety building about the many tasks I still had to accomplish and the need to get on the road so as not to be late for my next appointment. Closing out my computer, I grabbed my keys and ran to my car, barely stopping to put on my seatbelt before pulling out of the parking lot. As I rounded the corner, I was confronted with a multitude of ambulances and fire trucks—all of which surrounded a car that had flipped over and was barely recognizable. Pulling over to the side of the road, I took a deep breath, gathered my thoughts, and said a quick prayer for those involved. While being on time is important, nothing is ever worth risking your life or the lives of others in order to get there faster.

I share this story because I spoke on the phone this morning with someone who was very focused on "time." Since the death of her loved one, she couldn't help but play back in her mind all of the times they had spent together enjoying each other's company. What she couldn't shake off was all of the times when they had the opportunity to make time for one another but didn't for whatever reason. Regrets like these ring true within so many relationships and family systems. Time becomes an adversary for those who are dying and are eager for more of it, and it becomes a friend to those who are suffering and are hoping for a quick and merciful end.

For those of us left behind, we can choose to look at the time we had with our loved ones as a gift—honoring the memory of our loved one and all that we hold so dear about them. However, when we are grieving, it is difficult to be thankful or grateful, instead we blame time for being stingy, never giving enough of itself to satisfy our needs. I've observed as husbands watched their wives (and vice versa) from hospital beds as if soaking up every single moment, not wanting to sleep for fear of losing what precious time they have left. For them, it feels like the ticking of the clock is louder than a passing train, with each second a reminder that they are closer to that final moment. Once that second, that minute, that hour, that day is gone, we are struck with the intimate knowledge that time escapes us when we take it for granted.

What some of us realize after the death of a loved one is that the overall emotional experience can give us the opportunity to take time for ourselves, to examine where we are in life and sincerely look at what our future holds. Maybe we are more open about our feelings or more present with our loved ones; or maybe we are kinder in our words and actions, or more willing to make some changes. We are acutely aware that if we blink our eyes, our children will be grown or we will be closer to retirement, but never once stop to enjoy the life that we are living. Our world is very fast paced and only seems to slow down when tragedy occurs. Shouldn't we become more cognizant of our many blessings—of the life we are currently living?

When people say "time is of the essence," it is a prompting that we simply cannot delay or put off things we "meant to do or meant to say." If we get into this habit, our grief will play havoc on our emotions and literally slam us to the ground in its harsh reminder that we had been given time to engage in our life, or in the lives of others, but instead made decisions that will impact our grief journey. So, have those conversations; keep those appointments; give of yourself even when you are exhausted. Time is precious—don't put off until tomorrow what you can do today, but remember to slow down. Racing through life will only bring you closer to the finish line and because of that, you may be more likely to miss out on the life you are living.

Pay it Forward

By now, we've all seen the TV commercials where a bystander notices someone do something nice for someone else, thus inspiring them to do something nice for another person. In theory, as this is witnessed by the next individual, another nice act is set into motion, creating a series of events that promote kindness and the act of reaching out to others. When we find ourselves walking down the grief path, we are often recipients of these acts of kindness. People show up at our door with homemade casseroles, cakes, and warm hugs. They call us throughout the day to check and see how we are doing or if we need anything, and our mailboxes are full of sympathy cards and best wishes. What eventually happens is that the bereaved often experience the tapering off of those acts of kindness to a small trickle of support. The food stops arriving, the calls eventually slow down, and the cards in the mailbox all but disappear. As the friends and family of those who are newly bereaved, I want to encourage you to find ways in which you can continue to find ways to be present and supportive. What can we do?

Nothing breaks my heart more than finding someone who is on their grief journey and their support is severely limited. Maybe they have family but they live out-of-state; maybe they don't belong to a church community; or maybe they have simply lost contact with neighbors and friends. When our support is limited, when we don't have someone present in our lives to help alleviate some of our grief, the weight becomes extremely heavy and unbearable. I would like to think that in our community, we have people who are blessed with the gift of selflessly giving to others. They constantly look for ways they can reach out to someone who is hurting and do something simple and meaningful to brighten their day.

I have witnessed this—the selfless giving of time, energy, and sometimes money. I have seen people show up at someone's home and mow their lawn, rake their leaves, and water their plants. I have watched as others have baked cakes for birthdays or anniversaries that are still meaningful to the bereaved—the tears flowing from their eyes as they realize that their loved ones have not been forgotten, even in death. At other times, I have seen money slid into envelopes, an anonymous gift to help someone who is struggling with paying the bills since their loved one has died. All of these acts are powerful and mean so much to those who are receiving them. What is often overlooked is that when we participate in these acts of kindness, it lifts our own spirits and places an extra bounce in our step. Due to the fast-paced world we live in, we sometimes create a sense of "business" that allows us to excuse our ability to reach out to those around us. If we take the time to slow down and recognize that our simple actions can go a long way toward making a true difference in a person's life, we would be surprised at how rewarding it feels to help someone else.

I have been encouraging the bereaved in our community to focus some of their "love energy" on a skill or task that they enjoy—whether that is baking, woodworking, gardening, etc. By thinking of their loved ones and focusing their grief in the direction of "paying it forward" they can in turn reach out to others who are newly bereaved. This gesture tends to be meaningful because it is coming from their heart—for they have been there and are currently walking along the same path. To be the recipient of a gift such as this is an incredible feeling, just as the giving of this gift is a treasure that was simply waiting to be discovered. When we touch the living soul of another and witness their radiant joy, our souls cannot help but sing. Reach out and touch someone today—it will change your life forever.

Keep the Fire, Live to Inspire

We have all been there before, staring blankly down the barrel of life with no response or action to give back. Sometimes it is rather difficult to plod onward day in and day out, always living our life with purpose. Friends, family, and coworkers look to us for positive role modeling, often shaping their actions based simply on what we are doing or how we are presenting our feelings. At times, always setting a good example becomes draining and tiresome. What happens when we have a terrible, no good, rotten, very bad day? How do we manage to push forward and live to inspire those around us?

First and foremost, it is about taking care of ourselves. Human nature dictates that we should have a "place others first" mentality. We are taught to serve others and make a difference in their lives, providing energy and direction. However, I am of the belief that if we don't take the time to put ourselves first every once in a while, the energy we have to give will be depleted. It is of utmost importance to take care of ourselves, to engage in some every day "self-maintenance" in order for us to truly be there for others. Because we are human, and because most of us try to live our lives absent of self-need and selfishness, this can become a challenge. When asked to take a realistic look at ourselves and how we are taking care of our bodies and our minds, we are often hard pressed to find what it is exactly we do for our own health maintenance.

Let's start with a simple task, one that we don't think about and are only aware of when it is called to our attention: Breathing. Breathing is an automatic response, one that is constantly practiced and one that carries us forward in life—for without breath, we are simply "not alive." By learning to focus on our breathing, we can slow down our automatic "fight or flight" response when confronted with an uncomfortable event, which allows us to process with a clearer mind, and thus make more informative and collective decisions. Harnessing our own inner strength and being the pilot of our own breathing can change the way we respond, and more often than not, it projects a positive nature.

Once we have accomplished this task, it is necessary to look at our "frame of mind." In order to be a positive influence on others or to influence mindful change, we must believe in the positive. Of course, always looking on the bright side of things, or turning negatives into positives, is not always possible in uncertain times. The challenge we have in our everyday lives, is to maintain some semblance of certainty, as it will affect our mood and our presentation to others. By changing the way we look at life, by having a willful determination to look negativity in the eye and illicit positive change, we create change in not only ourselves, but in the collective thoughts and actions of others as well.

Once we have become well practiced in our breathing and frame of mind, we must take a look at an "action plan." Reading about things and thinking about them while never making a determined effort to engage in change can be detrimental to our health. It is common knowledge that when we become a positive influence on others, it creates tremendous joy within. Our energy level grows stronger, we are more full of life. The longer we function on this level, the more the effect on our inner selves. We create an abundance of energy that we can tap into when we are not feeling our best. The reciprocal effect is that others will respond in kind—a positive action creates a positive reaction. If we wish to be treated fairly and kindly, with respect and dignity, we must do our best to treat others this way, and to live our lives so as to inspire those around us. When others observe our actions, it creates change—either positive or negative. We do not live in a vacuum, nor is our life meaningless or unobserved. We are the creators of our own paths; we are the pilots of our own lives.

Taking care of ourselves, so we can stoke the fires of passion and change, is essential to being a source of inspiration to others. If we can devote time to a dedicated mindfulness of building positive energy by focusing on taking care of ourselves, then we are well on our way to role modeling effective behavior for others. We make a living statement that we are resolved to harness the fire within ourselves; that this fire will burn brightly and forcefully; and will be visible to those around us. Once we master the art of our inner flame, our daily path then becomes one of inspiration. Keeping the fire so we can live to inspire is a healing action—not only for others, but for our own inner peace. Burn brightly.

Community Feedback

"I just wanted to send you a quick note to say that I absolutely love reading your column each week. Some days I shed tears as I can relate to a lot of the things you talk about. My grandmother passed away twelve years ago and she was like a mother to me. At that time, my children were small and my mom was having a hard time dealing with it, so I kind of suppressed all my grief in order to help everyone else. It has only been recently that I've been able to 'slow down' in my life and think back on my grandmother and finally be able to grieve … twelve long years of holding it in! Anyway, I just wanted to let you know how much of an impact your columns make on the local folks who read it—I've even heard several people in the area comment on it. Kudos to you for finding your calling."

"Your article was 'on target' for so many. Keep up the writing style so that we readers can seem to feel that we are in the space that you are describing."

"My mother died recently and I was moved by how beautifully you described the quiet days before the soul leaves the body. Mom had a severe stroke five days before her death, so we were not able to hear her say goodbye. She had expressed her love fully every day, so we didn't feel the lack. My brother and I spent time with her one at a time, so on my turn I got to do all the talking, alternating talking with singing and sweet silence. I was there at the end, and I had the transcendent experience of singing her away, singing the lullaby my dad's mother sang to him, and taught mom in turn. All my girls sing the song to their children. I am telling you this because we had wonderful hospice attendants with us. They were so kind and so helpful in letting us know what was happening and how the end would draw near. They let us have privacy in her bedroom, but were right outside. I know that you know you have a heavenly privilege as you assist the family to say goodbye. Thank you for expressing it so well. Blessings!"

"For sure, there are angels on this earth that we can see and touch and who walk among us … the healthy, sick, dying, grieving, young, old … you are one of those angels. God gave you special gifts and a special spirit that you are sharing with the world of the suffering, dying and grieving. I have laminated your article so that forever I can be reminded that we all hope to walk that path of dying and dignity and an angel is beside us."

"I loved your word 'welcome' because that's what we do with our members—we want them to feel a part of our group and that we all understand, even though our child may have died in a different way at a different age. Your point that people don't want to listen and that they want to fix things they see wrong in those of us who are grieving was right on target. So many of our newly bereaved feel that their own families don't want to listen to their issues after a few months and just tell them that they need to 'move on.' Seriously? It's hard enough to deal with the loss of your precious child and then have to explain to family and friends what you are dealing with and then they won't listen. Thank you for writing and educating our community about grief. I do hope relatives and friends of the bereaved will listen instead of trying to fix them."

"I just read your column and wanted to let you know that I appreciated it very much. It was very helpful for me in helping family members who have lost their spouses. I was very moved by this one and just wanted to thank you for writing."

"This email isn't about anything in particular and I myself am only a passive reader, but I wanted to take the time to say that I was deeply moved by your article about the aging gentleman and his supportive wife. Conceptually, death isn't easy, nor is it calming, but you have a way with your words that not only exceeds that boundary, but helps to amplify it in an articulate manner. I hope that you continue writing articles and providing comfort for those who need it the most."

"I wanted to let you know I have enjoyed reading your articles. Thanks for sharing your knowledge and experience from your bereavement counseling. I believe that it has probably helped many people to see things in a new light in this area."

"Another spot on column! I'm working with a young mom whose young daughter recently died and you have so accurately described her feelings running into her friends. Keep up the good work!"

"You hit another one out of the ballpark! You so accurately described how my dad was after my mom died. So reading your article really touched me very much. Thank you for your beautiful words."

"I always look forward to reading your thoughts and learn from each article. Thanks so much for all that you do and for how deeply you care."

"Thanks so much for your wonderful articles on grief. I always look forward to them and save them for use with others who are dealing with that particular issue. I really appreciated your suggestion that people seek support and help. At a time of loss most people want to retreat and stay to themselves and that is when they need the most help. You are educating so many of us. Blessings!"

"I just read your article on child loss and am at a loss for words. I just wanted to say that this hit home and touched my heart. A few years ago, I prepared myself to welcome my grandchildren, twins, but due to unforeseen circumstances, my granddaughter died an hour after being born. My daughter was crushed and my heart was broken. You mentioned how sometimes these situations get overlooked, and they do. Thank you for your article."

"You did it again. Thank you so much for bringing this need to our attention by your thoughtful and compassionate description of the elderly who are isolated and feel forgotten. I'm saving this article so when I completely quit work, it can remind me of a need I just might be able to assist with."

"Thank you, thank you for such a precious and meaningful article. I recall so many special times with my husband and how he demonstrated just what you are writing about. Great job! One of your best!"

"I just loved your article on 'Animals: Grief and Unconditional Love.' One of the most tragic things for us are the older pets who are turned in when their owners have died. It is important that we all make provisions for our pets for when we are no longer able to care for them."

"You are doing a great job writing about a subject that touches us all. I can tell you are making a difference in people's lives."

"Thank you for the excellent article. It reminded me so much of how much I still miss breakfast with my wife every morning—I still feel her presence every day."

About the Author

Jenny Filush-Glaze is a licensed counselor who specializes in grief awareness and all aspects of death and dying. She is very passionate about supporting the bereaved and has found new ways to reach those who are grieving, primarily through "Grief Relief," the weekly column that runs in the *OA News* and *The Valley Times* (collected for you within the pages of this book); and *ZenJen's Cuppa Mourning Joe*, a blog that focuses on life, death, and positive healing.

An avid reader and a nature lover, she enjoys hiking, kayaking and just "being one with the great outdoors." She is currently the Bereavement Coordinator for a local hospice and is the founder and director of a children's grief camp that is held annually in order to support "our forgotten mourners," children who have experienced loss. She resides in Auburn, Alabama with her "Happy Family" and her many rescue dogs and lives each day with the goal of making a difference in the lives of others.

Jenny would enjoy hearing from you and is available for book talks. To share a message with her or to schedule her to speak to your group, please contact her at: grieftalksjfg@gmail.com.

CPSIA information can be obtained
at www.ICGtesting.com
Printed in the USA
FSHW020744231218
54416FS